Old World

New World

Craig Storti is available as a trainer/consultant in the subjects covered in this book. He can be reached at:

e-mail: cstorti@carr.org
Phone: 410-346-7336
Fax: 410-346-7846

Craig Storti is also the author of
The Art of Coming Home
The Art of Crossing Cultures
*Cross-Cultural Dialogues: 74 Brief Encounters with Cultural
    Difference*
Figuring Foreigners Out
Incident at Bitter Creek

Old World

Bridging Cultural Differences:
Britain, France, Germany, and the U.S.

New World

CRAIG STORTI

First published by Intercultural Press. For information contact:

Intercultural Press, Inc.
PO Box 700
Yarmouth, Maine 04096 USA
207-846-5168
Fax: 207-846-5181
www.interculturalpress.com

Nicholas Brealey Publishing
36 John Street
London, WC1N 2AT, UK
44-207-430-0224
Fax: 44-207-404-8311
www.nbrealey-books.com

© 2001 by Craig Storti

Production and cover design by Patty J. Topel

D
1065
.U5
S76
2001

Printed in the United States of America

05 04 03 02 01   1 2 3 4 5

Library of Congress Cataloging-in-Publication Data

Storti, Craig.
    Old World/New World: bridging cultural differences: Britain, France, Germany, and the U.S./Craig Storti
        p. cm.
    Includes bibliographical references (p.   )
    ISBN 1-877864-86-2
    1. Europe—Relations—United States. 2. United States—Relations—Europe. 3. Intercultural communication—Europe. 4. Intercultural communication—United States. 5. Ethnic attitudes—Europe. 6. Ethnic attitudes—United States. 7. National characteristics, American. 8. National characteristics, European. I. Title.
D1065.U5 S76 2001
303.48'24073—dc21   2001039398

Dedication

To Cha: Mother-in-law extraordinaire.

Table of Contents

Chapter 2: Americans and the French........................ 97

Dialogue/Analysis

Acknowledgments

As usual, the people at Intercultural Press saved me from the most egregious of my self-indulgent instincts. I tip my hat to David Hoopes for telling me some hard truths about the first draft of this book. Judy Carl-Hendrick is the kind of editor every writer dreams of having and never gets; they just don't make them like her anymore. Patty Topel's designs humble those of us who think it's really only the words that matter.

As for Toby Frank, I've used up my superlatives in earlier acknowledgments. She continues to be all those great things I have said she was, of course, just more so. As the years (and books) go by, I marvel that whenever I call her, she still makes me feel like she's got all the time in the world for me. That's called generosity of spirit, and they don't make much of *that* anymore either.

Introduction

*[It] was not the first nor the last time European thought
would prove inadequate to American realities.*
—Daniel J. Boorstin
The Americans: The National Experience

This book is about how Americans are different from Europeans—and in particular, how they are different from the British, the French, and the Germans. And vice versa. Cultural differences between Americans and Europeans complicate cross-cultural interactions and lead to all kinds of frustration and unpleasantness. And whether you calculate the costs in terms of crippled business ventures—by one estimate, 60 percent of all international joint ventures fail (Foster 1999, 14)—lost revenues, squandered opportunities, or just poor working relations, the price that companies and organizations and individuals pay for cultural misunderstanding is often too high. Becoming aware of cultural differences, however, can help eliminate such misunderstanding and all its possible effects.

Old World/New World has been written primarily for Americans who need to understand the British, French, and Germans better and for members of those three countries who need to understand Americans better. But it will also help people from other countries understand the featured cultures and, with any luck, teach people *from* these four countries a good deal about themselves.

Culture as the Problem

Why do cultural differences cause problems? Not all cultural differences do, of course; some of the different things foreigners do can be charming, ingenious, and otherwise perfectly agreeable. But some of their other traits are— pick your word—strange, offensive, maddening, or impossible. And these behaviors can be a nuisance. But why? Why should certain things the British do, for example, bother Americans so much? Or why should certain American behaviors irritate the French or the Germans?

People from different cultures have different values and beliefs—deeply ingrained ideas about what is right, good, normal, and natural—and these values and beliefs determine how those individuals behave and what they are supposed to say and do, as well as not say and not do, in various situations. As children we all learn and internalize the values and behaviors of our culture, what we might call the code of conduct in that society, until it becomes entirely natural and instinctive for us to behave in certain ways and to never behave in others. Needless to say, when people from different countries come in contact with each other—people who have learned two different codes of conduct—they are bound to say and do things that will confuse, frustrate, and offend each other. And the more this happens, the more often people from one country (e.g., the United States) offend or frustrate people from another (e.g., France), the harder it will be for them to live and work together. "[W]e are all subject in our thinking," David Hickson and Derek Pugh have written,

> at least to some degree, to "ethnocentrism." [This] is the implicit assumption, often unawares, that our culture is the best, that our way of doing things is normal, the right way.... We all overestimate the importance of our country and our culture in the scheme of things. When we see something different in another culture, we are liable to view it as abnormal and inferior....
>
> The development of this belief in our own culture is an important part of our ability to function effectively in it. But it is a feature of human nature which does lead to problems when we come to operate in other cultures. (1995, 253–54)

For this to change, for Americans and the French, for example, to be able to interact successfully, the Americans will need to see that certain behavior they perceive to be offensive in the French is in fact considered perfectly normal and acceptable to a French person. And vice versa. Each side, in other words, will have to realize that the so-called offensive behavior of people from the "other side" *is neither intended to offend nor considered offensive* in that person's own culture. Once that happens, once the parties to a cross-cultural "incident" understand that the other person does not mean to offend, they can usually get along. The particular behaviors may still strike the offended individuals as wrong or rude or just plain unnatural—they may still wish the other person would stop acting that way—but chances are they will no longer judge the perpetrator so harshly. That's the hope, anyway, and the idea behind this book.

What Is a Dialogue?

As used in this book, the word *dialogue* refers to a brief conversation between two people from different cultures, one from the United States and the other from one of the three European countries, wherein one or more cultural differences causes a misunderstanding. Each dialogue captures a cultural difference as it unfolds in a real situation. The dialogue is subsequently decoded in an analysis in the second half of the chapter, where the cultural difference is identified and explained at some length. In some of the dialogues, the speakers realize there has been a misunderstanding, but in most—just as in real-life cross-cultural encounters—they do not.

Each dialogue thus captures a cross-cultural "incident," an unsuccessful interaction which complicates or may even undermine relations between the two speakers. These incidents, as noted earlier, are the rocks on which most cross-cultural undertakings founder. In this book we don't actually see what these misunderstandings lead to, but it's not difficult to imagine: misinterpretations, erroneous assumptions, inaccurate conclusions. And these consequences, in turn, are responsible for the failure of a wide range of interpersonal, professional, and business relationships.

Let's examine a sample dialogue as an example of the dialogues and discussions presented in this book.

> NATASHA: Excuse me, but the elevator is out
> of order.
>
> SHARON: Really? Whom should we talk to?
>
> NATASHA: Talk to?
>
> SHARON: To report it.
>
> NATASHA: I have no idea.
>
> SHARON: Oh, I'm sorry; I thought you lived
> in this building, too.
>
> NATASHA: But I do.

In this exchange the cultural difference on display (if you can see it) is the activist, take-charge attitude of the American, Sharon, versus the more fatalistic, wait-and-see attitude of the Russian, Natasha. Sharon has been raised to believe that individual action can make a difference, that personal intervention of some sort on her part could actually lead to getting this elevator fixed. Natasha has been raised to believe that while individual action can sometimes bring results, there are many cases where it cannot—situations, that is, that are beyond the individual's ability to control or influence. Without getting into why Americans and Russians think so differently in this regard, we can see that each speaker is likely to go away from this conversation confused, perhaps even annoyed, by the attitude of the other speaker. Sharon goes away thinking Natasha is somewhat passive and defeatist, giving up too easily, and Natasha goes away thinking Sharon is rather naive and unrealistic to presume she can solve all the world's problems.

The point for the culture crosser to understand here is that while each speaker has responded to the situation very differently, each has also responded quite normally. The problem, of course, is that what is normal in their respective cultures is not the same. As a result, there's a good chance that the "normal" behavior of each speaker will in fact strike the other speaker as very odd. If you were to multiply such incidents, that is, if Natasha and Sharon were to repeatedly surprise each other with odd or frustrating behavior (they would probably call it "wrong" behavior), they would soon have serious doubts about each other. As mentioned above, we don't actually see the fallout from such incidents in these pages, but we see where and how things start to go sour because of cultural differences. In studying dialogues, then, we get to the bottom of the misinterpretations and mistaken judgments that cause so many cross-cultural relationships to fail.

Readers may feel that the cultural misunderstanding illustrated in the dialogue above was not especially obvious, that it could easily take a second or third reading even to see it. This is a deliberate feature of most of the dialogues in this book: the cultural mistake one or both speakers make is not readily apparent and may not become so until the reader turns to the analysis. This not only makes the dialogue a puzzle which the reader is then challenged to figure out, but the invisible nature of the mistake also accurately reflects real-life cross-cultural encounters, where the players are often not aware that a cultural difference has caused a misunderstanding. Indeed, if the two speakers in such an encounter *were* aware of their cultural differences, they would not be likely to misinterpret each other in the first place.

Why Dialogues?

Needless to say, it wasn't necessary to create dialogues in order to describe how Americans and Europeans are dif-

ferent. This book could have bypassed the cultural interactions altogether and simply presented the analyses as a
series of short essays on American/European cultural differences. It could simply have said, for example, that
Americans are direct and the British are indirect and then
explained the difference in some detail. But understanding cultural differences in the abstract is quite different
from recognizing and dealing with specific instances "in
the flesh." It's one thing to realize that Americans and the
British are different, and even to understand the nature of
those differences, but it's quite another to appreciate the
specific problems those differences can cause. So while you
may not need a dialogue to understand how a British person and an American are different, you do need dialogues
(or something like them) to bring such differences to life.
And it is only in life, after all, in actual instances of behavior, that cultural differences matter.

It Doesn't Have to Be Culture

Readers on occasion may feel that the misunderstanding
illustrated in a particular dialogue need not be the result
of a cultural difference. They might feel that two speakers
from the *same* culture could just as easily have this conversation, in which case the misunderstanding would then
have to be ascribed to some other dynamic, such as personal differences or class, gender, or age differences (to
name only a few). That is entirely possible, of course; our
point here is not that cultural differences are the *only* reason people misunderstand each other—would that they
were!—but that when people from different cultures fail
to communicate successfully, culture is always a *possible*
explanation and should never be ruled out.

In actual fact the opposite phenomenon is much more common: that is, people from two different countries who are in fact having a genuine *cultural* misunderstanding almost invariably assume that the problem is in fact something else—they usually think it's personal—because they don't know enough about culture to identify it as the problem.

Culture Is Relative

The reader should understand that when we make statements in these pages to the effect that the British are indirect, for example, or that Americans are blunt or that the French are formal, we are making comparative observations. The British are in fact indirect compared with many Americans, but the Japanese would probably not find them so. And while Americans may be blunt compared with the British, the Germans wouldn't necessarily agree (and Israelis most certainly would not). So it is that an American might want to be more understated around the British but would be well advised to speak more candidly to the Germans. All cultural characterizations, in short, have much more to do with the eye of the beholder than with the behavior of the beheld.

Cultural Similarities

For a dialogue as a cultural training tool to work—for it to *be* a dialogue—it must illustrate a cultural difference. Hence, this book is a catalogue of the ways the British, French, Americans, and Germans are different from each other, a virtual procession of misunderstandings, misinterpretations, and cultural faux pas. Bombarded by all these cultural differences, the reader might be forgiven for concluding that Americans and Europeans have nothing in common, that every time an American and a European talk to each other, there will automatically be some kind of misunderstanding or frustration.

But that's not the case. While Americans are indeed unlike the British, the French, and the Germans in fundamental ways, they are also like them in many other ways (the ways all people of European background are similar, for instance, as well as those ways that all people everywhere are alike—those universal values and behaviors we call human nature). But since these similarities don't usually lead to misunderstandings, they are not food for dialogues and are therefore not touched upon in these pages. It is important to acknowledge them, however, so that the reader does not get an exaggerated impression of the scale of European/American differences and, therefore, of how difficult it will be for these groups to get along.

Thanks to these cultural and universal similarities, then, it's entirely possible that when a German and an American interact, no cultural difference will arise and the entire encounter will go smoothly. Or, more likely, it means that some parts of the encounter will go well—those that do not involve a cultural difference—and some other parts may go poorly. In any case, readers can rest assured that not all cross-cultural interactions will be fraught with discomfort and frustration. Furthermore, they are not doomed to commit a faux pas every time they speak to a foreigner. If we do not focus on similarities in this book, therefore, it's not because we don't think they're important; it is, rather, because similarities by definition do not cause confusion and misunderstanding. And clearing up confusion and misunderstanding is our goal in these pages. To put it another way, people generally don't need help when interactions go well; they need help when interactions go badly.

Generalizations

Any book on culture, any book which seeks to describe entire groups of people, must necessarily rely on generalizations. While generalizing is a perfectly respectable way of organizing information, generalizations should not be made to carry more truth than they can bear. They are statements of the probable and the likely but not necessarily of the actual; they describe the typical, the normal, and the average but not always the real. By definition and by design, they transcend context; to generalize, after all, means to deliberately ignore the particular and the specific. But we should remember that nothing general ever happens, only specific events, nor does anything ever happen except *in context*. Moreover, there is no such thing as a general person, only unique individuals.

What are we to do with generalizations, then? Use them carefully. While all individuals are unique in many ways, they are also alike in other ways, and generalizations tell us how. They contain some truth; they are part of the story, but never the whole story. A cultural generalization can tell you how people from a particular culture *may* behave in a given situation but not necessarily how they *will* behave or how they will *always* behave. In the end, what a particular individual does in a particular situation will depend in part on culture and in part on the circumstances. Or, to put this another way, a person's culture is *one* of the circumstances that will influence his or her behavior in any given situation.

John Mole, author of *Mind Your Manners: Managing Business Cultures in Europe*, makes another important point about generalizations. He embarked on his book, he says, with considerable misgivings about making general cultural observations.

> It was surprising, therefore, to discover how consistent observations [about people from other cultures] were from people different in nationality, age, sex, and background. Whether or not they exist in reality, [cultural types] certainly exist in the perception of outsiders. And it is in perceptions of behavior that misunderstandings occur. (1995, 11)

Who Is an "American?"

The United States is becoming an increasingly culturally diverse society, making it more difficult to offer accurate generalizations about "American culture." A word is in order, then, about how the term *American** is used in these pages.

The type of individual most likely to exhibit the collection of cultural characteristics labeled "American" in this book is a white man or woman of European descent. While Americans of other backgrounds would manifest some or even most of these same cultural attributes (and many white Americans of European descent might *not* identify with some of these characteristics), white Americans are nevertheless the *group* of individuals in whom these attributes are the

---

* *America* is also used in this book to refer to the United States. Although there are differing views about the propriety of using this term, it is regularly used by Europeans and has thus been retained here.

most commonly found. African Americans, for example, share many of these same attributes, as do Americans of Hispanic origin, to name the two largest minority populations in the United States, but these two groups also exhibit various other cultural characteristics not widely associated with Americans of European descent. Moreover, when a western European uses or reads the word *American* to describe the culture of the U.S., he or she is more likely to be thinking of Euro-Americans than any other group, whether consciously or unconsciously.

On a related note, the phrases "American experience," "American history," and "American national experience" (or sometimes just "national experience") are also used frequently in these pages. Once again, the experience we are referring to in these phrases is that of the typical U.S. citizen of European descent. It goes without saying that the histories and cultures of other groups who either lived in America (Native Americans) or came to America— African Americans, for example, or Hispanics and Asians—are fundamentally different from the history of European Americans. While these other national experiences are as much a part of the culture of the United States as any, they are not by and large the experiences that have created the characteristics we refer to as American in these pages. If we do not mention these other histories here, therefore, it is not because they are any less American but only because they fall outside the scope of this undertaking. An interesting set of dialogues could certainly be written depicting differences between African Americans and the French, for example, or Hispanic Americans and the Germans, but that is a book for another day.

"But I'm Only Going to London"

Some readers may wonder if this book is really necessary: "I'm only going to London, not Ethiopia." Whenever a European goes to America or an American goes to Europe, there is a sense that one is headed for a destination that is somehow not all that foreign. Oh, the food may be different and the language, of course, but it's not like going to China or Borneo. What differences there are, surely, are differences in degree but not in kind.

There is some truth in this observation in the sense that Europeans and Americans are probably more like each other than either is like the Japanese, let's say, or the Egyptians. Americans came from Europe, after all—they *were* Europeans not so long ago—and while they evolved and became their own people after they arrived in the New World, much that was European inevitably survived. There is the common cultural heritage, for example, the Greco-Roman and the subsequent Judeo-Christian influence as well as geographic similarity. Europe and the United States are both northern regions with similar climates and vegetation, Europeans and Americans are both Caucasian, and their houses and buildings are similar. If we use the analogy of music, Americans and Europeans are variations on a theme, whereas Germans and the Chinese, for example, are two different themes altogether.

This notion of Euro-American sameness is a useful observation, then, but it would be a mistake to make too much of it. There are also numerous and significant differences between the Old World and the New; enough to call this book into being. Moreover, a good case can be made for the argument that cultures that are *somewhat* different from one's own may in fact pose more problems for the culture crosser than those that are wholly different. The European-American similarities that do exist, it might be argued, may cause both sides to assume or project still more similarities that most assuredly do not exist. Surface similarities in particular can fool the unsuspecting into presuming beneath-the-surface sameness that is nowhere to be found. Thus it is that Americans and Europeans visiting each other's side of the Atlantic or working together often let down their guard and are less alert to differences than they would normally be in a "more foreign" country—with predictable results. "It is always a jolt for veteran [American] travelers," Mort Rosenblum has written, "to find that culture shock in France is more severe than in Saudi Arabia or Bolivia. Elsewhere, things look and sound different, so you expect them to be different. [But] France looks like home, or at least like familiar old postcards and paintings. Surprise" (1988, 25). In short, the difficulty of adjusting to another culture may not be so much a function of how different that culture is from your own but how different it is from what you were *expecting*.

Be that as it may, we can rest assured that whether or not the American in Europe or the European in America has in fact entered a whole new world, he or she has most definitely gone to a foreign country. And this book, as a consequence, may be necessary after all.

A New World

It's still a fair question, however, how Americans, so recently Europeans themselves, could evolve into a culture and a people so different from their forebears, how this child of Europe could grow up to be so unlike its parents. This question deserves a few moments of our time.

America did not merely turn out to be different from Europe by default; it was different by design. Americans may indeed have come from Europe, but that's just the point: they left. And Europeans did not. There were things about life in Europe that made those who chose to emigrate unhappy or dissatisfied, things they wanted to get away from. We can therefore be quite sure that whatever those things were, Americans neither re-created nor tolerated them in the New World. Immigrants didn't leave the safety and security of home and sail across the North Atlantic to utterly alien shores merely to re-create there a way of life they had found unbearable in Europe.

Part of what makes America American, then, is that many of its basic values and traditions came about expressly in reaction to what made Europe European. If it was religious intolerance people were escaping, then religious tolerance would take its place in America. If they were escaping the rigid and oppressive class system, then the ideal would be a culture free of inherited rank and privilege. "The whole of the American experience," John McElroy writes, "was opposed to the social beliefs of Europe's aristocratic culture" (1999, 160). In his book, O Strange New World, Howard Mumford Jones itemizes the many ways America was the antithesis of Europe: "The United States had no monarch, no hereditary aristocracy, no tradition of culture, no landed gentry enjoying the right of primogeniture, no established church, no secret police, no royal council of state, no house of peers, no 'society,' and no feudal tenure..." (1968, 295–96).

But America is much more than merely *not* Europe; it is also its own place. It is, in other words, as much a result of what the immigrants found in the New World as it is a reaction to what they left behind in the Old. The physical place itself was astonishing to the average European, teeming with forests, game and fish, rivers, and natural resources—and land, endless land, the phenomenon that shaped American culture more than any other single factor and the one most responsible for making America so different from Europe. To the average European immigrant, endless land that was also practically devoid of people (as America was by European standards) was reality turned upside down. "For centuries," Carl Degler writes,

> the problem in Europe had been that of securing enough land for the people, but in the New World the elements in the equation were reversed…. The possibility of exaggeration should not hide the undeniable fact that in early America, and through most of the nineteenth century, too, land was available to an extent that could appear only fabulous to land-starved Europeans. (1984, 2)

But Americans were not only determined to make the United States different from Europe, they were also determined to make it superior. And not only to Europe, actually, but to anyplace history had seen so far. From the beginning America represented a chance to design from scratch a new paradigm, a noble experiment to build on the lessons of history—the false starts and wrong turns of their predecessors as well as their achievements—and establish not just a new country or a new land but a New World. America would be the place where civilized man finally got it right. "America seemed indecently optimistic," Richard Pells writes, "a country that believed itself to be 'immune from most human ills' and 'to have conquered most human problems'" (1997, 11).

It was natural [Pells continues] for Americans, as people who had escaped the political, religious, or economic constraints of Europe, to think of them-selves and their environment as unique. The rheto-ric of the earliest Puritan sermons portrayed America as a new promised land, a City Upon a Hill, a chance to start over and do it better, a model community for the rest of the world to emulate.

[T]he United States was a gigantic political and economic laboratory in which the libertarian and egalitarian ideals of the eighteenth century revo-lutions could be tested, modified, improved, and implemented.... (5)

This obligation to create a perfect society was another fac-tor making Americans almost instinctively suspicious of anything too European.

"A Race of Races"

Another factor in the evolution of a distinctly American culture was the great variety of nationalities among the early immigrants. English government policy put no re-strictions on who could immigrate to the American colo-nies (unlike the other colonial players, who often restricted immigration to their own citizens). Thus, America was settled by emigrants from a bewildering multitude of coun-tries, including England, Ireland, Scotland, Wales, Ger-many, France, Holland, Finland, and Sweden (and, later, emigrants from numerous countries in southern and east-ern Europe). "By the mid-eighteenth century," McElroy has noted, "the European ancestry of most Americans was so mixed that they were no longer Englishmen or [people] of any European 'race.' They had become what the American poet Walt Whitman was to call 'a race of races'" (27–28).

Back home in their respective countries, these people grew up and lived among people of their own kind and may never have encountered someone from a different culture. Suddenly, in the New World, they were surrounded by foreigners, by people unlike themselves, with different customs, traditions, values, beliefs and behaviors, and often languages. And yet together—for if not together, then not at all—they had to clear the land, plant crops, build homes, form communities, and govern themselves. In the process, in the daily collision of cultural traditions, values, and customs, there had to be give-and-take, compromise, and tolerance. To get along, indeed to survive, these early settlers quickly learned to overlook the frustrating, shocking, and "wrong" behavior of their neighbors. Thus were the sharpest edges of each nationality slowly worn down and rubbed smooth, until before very long the only word left to accurately describe these people—and their hybrid culture—was *American*.

*   *   *

These, then, are some of the reasons why Americans are so unlike their European ancestors, explanations for why the New World turned out to be not only superficially but also fundamentally different from the Old. These themes will reappear in the following chapters in various guises, helping to explain why Americans and the British, French, and Germans don't always understand each other.

1

Americans and the British

Dialogues 1–17

Once, from behind a closed door, I heard a British woman exclaim with real pleasure, "They are funny, the Yanks!" And I crept away and laughed to think a British person was saying such a thing. And I thought: They wallpaper their ceilings! They put little knitted bobble hats on their soft-boiled eggs to keep them warm! They don't give you bags in supermarkets! They say sorry when you step on their toes! Their government makes them get a hundred-dollar license every year for watching television! They charge you for matches when you buy cigarettes! They live in Barking and Dorking and Shellow Bowells! They have amazing names, like Mr. Eatwell and Lady Inkpen and Major Twaddle and

Miss Tosh! And they think we're funny?
> —Paul Theroux
> *The Kingdom by the Sea*

Many readers will naturally assume that of the three cultural pairings in this book, the Americans and the British have the most in common. They share a common language, after all, and the United States was once known as the "British colonies," boasting more emigrants from England than from any other country. There has to be some reason they go around calling each other cousins—something, it should be noted, that Americans and the French or Americans and the Germans never do.

While American and British cultures may be similar in some respects, the common language does nothing to advance the cause. Speaking the same language merely means that Americans and the British understand each other's words, but it hardly guarantees they understand each other's meaning. And it says nothing about whether their two cultures are alike; Indians speak English too, as do Jamaicans and Fijians, but no one would call them cultural kinfolk of the British.

Many immigrants to the colonies did indeed come from England, but immigrants are not necessarily representative of the country they leave behind, to say nothing of how they are transformed in their adopted homeland after their arrival. There is even some question as to whether England can in fact claim to have sent more immigrants to America than any other country. John Ardagh has pointed out that if you exclude the Irish, Welsh, and Scots, more early immigrants to America were actually of German than British origin. Indeed, British immigration policy permitted people from any country to settle in the colonies, so long as they paid their taxes, with the result that the British colonies were really British in name only. As John McElroy has observed, the colonies were so "mixed in European nationalities and Christian denominations... that such distinctions as Englishman and Frenchman began to lose their significance" (1999, 28).

And as we noted in the Introduction, paradoxically, cultural similarities often make cross-cultural interaction *more* difficult rather than less because of unmet expectations. In short, there is little reason for the reader to believe that Anglo-American interactions are going to be significantly easier than Franco-American or German-American interactions. Indeed, most observers would probably say that Americans are more like Germans than they are like either the British or the French. (Going further afield, Europeans often cite the Dutch as the culture most like the United States.) Neither the British nor the Americans should let their guard down, then, when they go to each other's country or when they work together. If anything, they should be more watchful than ever, so easy is it to be lulled by the sound of a familiar tongue into assuming all manner of other similarities that do not exist.

Class Matters

While the British are not of one mind on the subject, most non-British observers agree that social class still plays a prominent role in British culture (see Dialogue 6, "Moving Up," page 25). In talking about "the British," therefore, as we do at some length in these pages, it becomes necessary to specify which people one has in mind. In this book the cultural characteristics we have identified as British are most closely associated with the upper and upper-middle classes in that country and would not necessarily be true of the lower-middle and working-class sectors of the population. Indeed, in some ways the gulf between the British working class and the British upper class is nearly as wide as that between the British and the Americans.

Dialogues

1. Bad News

SUSAN: Poor Nigel.

ARABELLA: What happened?

SUSAN: The meeting was a bust. We didn't get the new funding.

ARABELLA: Did Nigel say something?

SUSAN: He didn't have to. It was written all over his face.

ARABELLA: Oh, dear.

2. Upgrade

MARK: There's a newer version of that software, you know.

COLIN: You're kidding! Already?

MARK: Came out just a month ago.

COLIN: This one is great.

MARK: The upgrade has a lot of new features.

COLIN: I'll bet.

MARK: Shall I order it for you?

3. A New Director

MIRANDA: It's between Price and Weston, I think, for the director position.

SHARON: Who do you think will get it?

MIRANDA: I've thought a lot about Price. He's extremely devoted to his work and quite serious about it.

SHARON: Yes. He's very conscientious.

MIRANDA: He's enthusiastic and gets quite worked up.

SHARON: Yes. I favor Price too.

4. Rewrite

CAROL: So, what did you think of the rewrite?

HUGH: Oh, yes, the rewrite. Are you pleased with it?

CAROL: Quite. Shall I send it down for printing, then?

HUGH: Up to you, really.

5. Dropping By

DEBBIE: You're the new man who just got back from Singapore?

ADRIAN: Yes. I don't think we've met. I'm Adrian Barnes.

DEBBIE: Debbie Young. Have you found a house yet?

ADRIAN: Yes. In Hampton, on Surrey Street.

DEBBIE: We live in Hampton, too. We love to walk in that park near you.

ADRIAN: It's very nice, isn't it?

DEBBIE: What's your street number? We'll drop by one of these days.

ADRIAN: Of course. We'll be getting our phone in next week.

DEBBIE: We'll help you unpack your boxes!

6. Moving Up

TODD: There's a vacancy in middle management, you know.

ARTHUR: I heard. I wonder who they'll select.

TODD: Why don't you apply? I've heard you're management's favorite shop foreman.

ARTHUR: I suppose I am, keeping the peace here on the floor.

TODD: So, you're tempted?

ARTHUR: Me? Are you kidding? I don't know any of those people.

TODD: But you've worked here for years.

7. All the Stops

AMANDA: I think the handwriting's on the wall here.

TOM: There just has to be a way to do this.

AMANDA: Can you honestly think of something we haven't tried?

TOM: Not really.

AMANDA: We did our best. Don't forget, no one else has ever pulled this off either.

TOM: But I'm not a quitter.

AMANDA: Neither am I.

8. Calling a Cab

ANN: Wow! It's 8:30. This was above and beyond the call of duty, I'd say.

ROWAN: All in a day's work, isn't it?

ANN: A very long day.

ROWAN: Doesn't happen that often anyway.

ANN: Our cab should be downstairs in 5 minutes. What do you say we charge it to the company?

ROWAN: You called a cab?

9. Office Mates

ROGER: What's with Blanchard?

JULIA: He's not himself, is he? I don't really know.

ROGER: You must know him pretty well, after all the time you've worked here together.

JULIA: We've been colleagues for a year, if that's what you mean.

ROGER: It is.

JULIA: It must be something personal. Marital problems, perhaps?

ROGER: I don't think so. He and I have shared an office for eight months now. I'd know if it was something like that.

10. Well Done

BOB: You did a fabulous job on that report.

MARTIN: We did our best. I wish we'd had more time.

BOB: For what? It really couldn't have been better.

MARTIN: I wouldn't like to think so.

BOB: You mean you left something out?

MARTIN: Excuse me?

11. Buying Blind

KAREN: Did you hear? Symonds Plc is coming on the market?

DEREK: I did. Quite unexpected.

KAREN: There's going to be a lot of interest.

DEREK: I've heard it could sell in less than a month. Some Americans are apparently quite keen.

KAREN: I know.

DEREK: I think it's what they call "buying blind."

KAREN: Doesn't give us much time.

DEREK: To do what?

KAREN: Get together our bid.

12. Vacancy

SIMON: Don, come in. What's up?

DON: I just heard there was a vacancy opening up in Finance.

SIMON: Yes. Claudia's leaving next month.

DON: I'd be interested in applying.

SIMON: Great. I've been mulling over possible candidates.

DON: I have an accounting background, you know.

SIMON: I think I did know that.

DON: Anyway, I hope you'll keep me in mind.

SIMON: I certainly will.

13. Sweet Time

TED: Nicholas. I'm glad I caught you.

NICHOLAS: I was just about to lock up.

TED: I just got off the phone with the lab.

NICHOLAS: Oh? Is it still raining outside?

TED: I think so. The guys in the lab said they've come up with a new coating that could cut our costs in half.

NICHOLAS. Really? Walk with me to the elevator.

TED: We've got to get the word out to plant managers.

NICHOLAS: Of course.

TED: Shall I start calling around?

14. Business Major

PENELOPE: Was that your son with you at the airport?

ANNA: Yes. He was visiting for the holidays but now he's going back to school in America.

PENELOPE: What does he want to do after college?

ANNA: He wants to go into business.

PENELOPE: What's he studying, then?

ANNA: Business.

PENELOPE: But what courses is he taking?

ANNA: Business courses, I imagine.

15. Looking Good

BILL: I think it's the best acquisition opportunity to come our way in years.

NILES: Looks good from a distance, that's for sure.

BILL: It's almost too good to be true—a complementary product line, seasoned management, a good financial package, and an expanding market. How can we miss?

NILES: Makes you wonder where the catch is, doesn't it?

BILL: Have you signed the letter of intent yet?

NILES: Too early for that, I'm afraid.

BILL: Is there a problem?

NILES: Nothing we've come across so far.

BILL: Great. I can't wait to work with those people.

16. Low Key

ROGER: What should we say to the Denton Group about their proposal, then?

REBECCA: That we're impressed, but there are one or two problems.

ROGER: One or two? It's full of problems!

REBECCA: Quite so. It needs a complete redo.

ROGER: Then we've got to tell them.

REBECCA: Of course.

17. Taking Advantage

CARL: I heard BMG's fourth quarter sales are going to be lower than expected.

CAMILLA: Yes. Their share price will probably drop. Makes it a bit sticky for them, doesn't it?

CARL: I think we should delay the merger discussions.

CAMILLA: To give us an advantage in the negotiations, you mean?

CARL: Right.

CAMILLA: And then we would be in a position to dictate the terms of the merger?

CARL: Exactly.

Analyses, Dialogues 1–17

1. Bad News

For every culture there is at least one characterization that becomes an enduring cliché: enduring because it is so apt, a cliché because it is so commonplace. With the British, it is the stiff upper lip, the cultural proscription against displaying one's emotions in public or, as the British call it, their "unflappability." Unchecked emotions are thought to lead too easily to chaos, or at the very least to unpleasantness, which is much the same thing. And the more charged the circumstances—the hotter the hot water one is in—the greater the necessity to stay calm. In any situation calling for emotional self-control, then, what matters above all else is keeping one's dignity. Or, as the British are likely to put it, whether or not you crack. Simply stated, if you're British, you must never crack. It's true, no doubt, that even British upper lips quiver now and then in the right circumstances, but such sightings are far too rare to undermine the cultural stereotype. "The British reputation for reserve is deserved," Timothy Harper has written. "Public displays of emotion would be frowned upon, if frowning itself wasn't a display of emotion" (1997, 23).

As the dialogue unfolds, Arabella has a growing suspicion that Nigel may have violated this important British norm. Upon learning that Nigel is upset, Arabella is concerned to find out just how obvious he was about his feelings, fearing that he may have lost his cool in front of his colleagues and superiors. When she asks, "Did Nigel say something?" she's trying to discover if he actually put his distress into words or, as she hopes (and as the culture prescribes), kept it to himself. She's not encouraged, therefore, when Susan says he didn't have to verbalize his feelings, they were "written all over his face." Arabella's concluding "Oh, dear" is not in fact what Susan thinks it is, sympathy for poor Nigel. It is, rather, a lament that Nigel lost control of his emotions in public, thereby embarrassing himself and perhaps even the division they all work for.

The unmoving upper lip is, of course, a stand-in for self-control, one of the paramount British virtues. Self-control, after all, is the key to civility, and civility is the cornerstone of British public life. So long as people are civil to one another, so long as they keep their emotions in check and don't get carried away, there won't be any "scenes," which are the ultimate British nightmare. "This reticence [in showing emotion] may be connected to the shyness of the British," Peter Collett writes, "but it probably has more to do with that cardinal rule which says that one must not make a scene in public. This desire not to cause any trouble is a very powerful motivating force in British life—one which sometimes threatens to be more important than life itself" (in Hill 1995, 67). In his book on the House of Windsor, Donald Spoto described the instinctive reserve of the British upper classes:

Their reticence derived from the formalities of Victorian society and the concomitant requirements of polite discourse. It was bred partly, too, in the ordinary British bone. One simply did not express any feeling with much enthusiasm. (Queen Victoria, sick with grief when [her husband] fell ill, noted simply in her journal that his absence from Christmas festivities was "tiresome.") Fervent words or spirited gestures might offend the sensibilities of others; the naked expression of sentiment was the way of the ill-bred commoner. (1995, 59)

The code for this emotional control among the British, incidentally, is the phrase "good manners," which has very little to do with knowing which is the salad fork and a great deal to do with understanding the necessity of always staying composed in public. Having good manners, it should be noted, is the primary requisite of a gentleman, and the gentleman and gentlewoman are supposed to be models for the less fortunate.

This cultural trait surely owes something to the great British tradition of stoicism, of suffering in silence and cheerfully coping with adversity. If you believe, as the British do, that life is going to be a struggle (the creed of the stoic), then clearly we all have to be tough. We can't very well lose our cool every time there's a setback, for example, as there are going to be rather a lot of them along the way. If we can't change the human condition, in other words, then we must endure it graciously. Emotional restraint may also have been a consequence of the class system, where you learned to hide your true feelings (especially negative ones) for fear of offending your betters upon whose goodwill and generosity you depended for your well-being.

Why does Susan miss most of what has occurred in the dialogue? Why doesn't she see the embarrassment, however slight, that Nigel has brought upon himself and feel bad for him? And why will she be surprised, moreover, when Nigel upbraids her (politely, of course) for telling Arabella about his unfortunate behavior? Largely because in Susan's culture Nigel hasn't done anything shameful and therefore has nothing to worry about. He didn't "lose it" (as Americans would say), after all, meaning he didn't actually say something or otherwise act upon his frustration or disappointment. More importantly, even if he had lost it, if he had given vent to his emotions and said what was on his mind, this behavior would normally not constitute a breach of decorum in America the way it does in England. Sounding off would not reflect badly on Nigel.

The whole view of emotions, and especially of controlling one's emotions in public, is quite different in the United States; indeed, the very idea of emotional self-control is something of an oxymoron to most Americans. To begin with, emotions are a natural, spontaneous phenomenon— they just happen—and Americans inherently trust what is natural. For Americans, then, emotions aren't inherently bad or dangerous, as they seem to be among the British, though Americans do accept that giving vent to emotions may be bad in the wrong circumstances. They realize that what is natural may not always be civil, in other words, but they believe strongly that civility purchased at the price of concealment and dishonesty, which is how Americans view the British attempt to suppress emotions, is a dubious achievement. Not surprisingly, Americans don't trust people who don't show any emotions, and they are especially critical of people who feel one emotion and display another (such as the British), finding such behavior wily and calculating.

Americans tend to regard emotional self-control as a kind of check on their independence, an infringement on their God-given right of self-expression. The freedom to express how one feels is almost as fundamental as the right to feel that way in the first place. This doesn't mean Americans can't control themselves or that they never hold their tongues (though they are often accused of just these offenses by Europeans), but that they are inclined to trust their feelings. They believe in the end that any unfortunate consequences of too much self-expression are still preferable to the consequences of excessive self-restraint. "Civility cannot be purchased from Americans on any terms," one nineteenth-century British visitor remarked. "They seem to think it is incompatible with freedom."

In the dialogue, then, Susan has no idea that she is delivering disappointing news to Arabella, much less that she is telling tales out of school about Nigel, for in her culture Nigel's behavior has been well within the bounds of propriety. As noted earlier, Nigel never actually *said* anything at the meeting, and so as far as Susan is concerned, he therefore has nothing to be embarrassed about. For the British, however, emotional self-restraint means more than just not verbalizing one's feelings; it means not showing them at all. The British, in short, distinguish between *having* emotions and *showing* them; the former is natural and unavoidable, but the latter is entirely a matter of self-discipline—of which you can never have too much as far as the British are concerned. Americans tend not to make this distinction; for them, having emotions *means* showing them. And the reverse is likewise true: people who don't show any emotions must therefore not have any or, worse, they're being coy.

In this context, Americans dealing with the British

should remember that whenever they feel they have stayed within the bounds of decorum as far as displays of emotions are concerned, the British may think they have crossed the line. Behavior that feels like self-control to an American, for example, may strike the British as rather emotional. For their part, the Arabellas of the world should realize that what constitutes good manners and reserve in their culture may come across to Americans as coldness and even as dissembling.

2. Upgrade

The British attitude toward the new, like their attitude toward so many things, is extremely practical. For the British, the newness of a thing does not automatically recommend it. Indeed, since the new is by definition untested and unproved, the only prudent response is to hold it suspect. It's not necessarily worse than whatever it might be replacing, but it's certainly not automatically better. Nor, for that matter, is it even necessarily new. In the end the only thing you can say for sure about the new is that it isn't old. The British are "relatively slow to put new ideas into practice," David Hickson and Derek Pugh have written. They "want to be sure something will work before leaping into it American style. They are wary of the future, more able to let things patiently work out" (1995, 58).

Hence Colin's reaction in the dialogue when he learns there is already an upgrade for the software he's using. If your attitude toward the new is to be skeptical and you're quite happy with the software you've got ("This one is great"), then you are going to be at best neutral when you hear there is a newer version. If you add to this the fact that it has probably taken Colin some time to master the present software ("Already?"), then you can be even more certain about his attitude toward the upgrade. The coup de grace, if one were needed, is Mark's comment that the upgrade "has a lot of new features." Even assuming that these new features are genuine enhancements, something a British person would not assume, Colin may be thinking of all the time it's apparently going to take him to master them. When Colin exclaims "You're kidding! Already?" it's not because he's starting to come around, to be persuaded by the force of Mark's argument, but merely to confirm the information about new features, which removes any doubt that the upgrade spells trouble for people like him. In the end, then, since new isn't necessarily better and since what he's got is working fine—since there's nothing broken here, nothing that needs fixing—just wherein lies the appeal of an upgrade? The answer to Mark's question, "Shall I order it for you?" should by now be clear even to Mark.

But it isn't, of course. In fact Mark is quite sure Colin will want the upgrade. Why does Mark miss all the cues? Quite simply, because Mark, like most Americans, has a very different take on things that are new. He has a deep and abiding faith in them, assuming that whatever is new is bound to be an improvement on what came before, inevitably a step forward. Or at the very least, worth a try. In America, Hickson and Pugh have observed, "...new ideas are to be tried in case they do work, rather than regarded skeptically because there is no evidence that they will work, which is the British inclination" (1995, 61). Americans have no more information about the new than anyone else, of course, no evidence or proof that it is in fact better; they just have their faith; they believe. For Mark, then, the mere existence of an upgrade is enough to make him want to try it. And the fact that it has new features is merely icing on the cake, for if these features are truly new, then they are bound to be enhancements.

What makes Americans such believers in the new? Their national experience, for one thing. From the beginning, America has been all about the new. You only went to America if you wanted something new, and you only survived there if you could cope with what you found. "The unexpected was the usual," Daniel Boorstin has written, "and men had to be ready for it" (1958, 193). Tradition, not surprisingly, was one of the first and greatest casualties of the American experience. What had always worked in Europe, the tried and true, often did not work in America or was simply irrelevant. Americans faced circumstances and problems Europeans had never encountered (the New World, Howard Jones writes, "was so incredibly filled with unpredictabilities, one wonders how the Europeans survived" [1968, 391]) and for which the European experience had no prescriptions of any kind, new or old. "To understand American culture," John McElroy has written, "one must always bear in mind that it developed from the situation of civilized men and women living in a Stone Age wilderness. Almost nothing in the cultural memory of the initial European settlers on the Atlantic coastal plain of North America prepared them for living in such a place" (1999, 17). In such situations tradition became suspect, something to question and doubt rather than something to rely on. Old ways of doing—to say nothing of thinking—only got in the way of "progress," which soon became the new American religion. Under the circumstances, to embrace the new was not so much an act of faith as it was a practical necessity.

In due course, Americans began to have good reason

to put their faith in the future, for their story soon became a series of successes, advances, and improvements (assuming you overlooked the odd anomaly, like the Civil War). Each succeeding generation lived better than its predecessors. Technological advances revolutionized transportation, communications, manufacturing, trade, and medicine. Abundant resources made life increasingly comfortable, and that level of comfort came to embrace more and more of the population. It is only natural Americans came to believe in what they called the march of progress, an unstoppable momentum toward a better and better world. The belief in progress, that newer was better, was not something Americans had to be converted to; it was a fact of everyday life.

So much progress and at such a breathtaking pace taught Americans that what was new didn't last very long; it was bound to be replaced by something still newer—and, of course, superior. In the time it takes for something new to begin to attract serious attention in Europe—Colin's trusty software, for example—such a thing will already be old and discarded in America.

The age of a culture may also affect its attitude toward new things. For young cultures, like young people, *everything* is new, and they tend to be more trusting and optimistic. Whether what is new is actually better is something that can only be known over time and with experience, and young cultures have had little of either. When you don't know any better, it's much easier to have faith.

The British national experience, meanwhile, has bred caution and skepticism. From the vantage point of ten or more centuries, the proverbial test of time, the new has not always turned out to be an improvement. Or even new. Nor has the march of progress always been in a forward direction; the human story, at least from the European perspective, is one of fits and starts, advances and reverses. What came next—the Black Death, the Inquisition, the Hundred Years' War, famine—was not always better than what came before. "Disunity and warfare have characterized the history of Europeans," McElroy has observed, while for "most Americans, history has been a foundation for further improvements" (1999, 74). Since the British experience of the new was so decidedly mixed, the only sensible approach to it was to be skeptical. At the end of the day (as the British say), new ideas, new technology, new ways of doing things have to be judged on their merits—and merely being new is not one of them.

Americans' uncritical acceptance of the new makes them come across as naive and unsophisticated to the British, and not entirely trustworthy as business partners. In the presence of their British cousins, then, Americans would do well to contain their enthusiasm for the untested. Meanwhile, the British might want to temper their caution and skepticism, which will likely strike Americans either as excuses for not wanting to change or as a sheer lack of imagination.

3. A New Director

It will come as a considerable surprise to Sharon that Miranda does not in fact favor Price for the director's job. What Miranda has intended as a list of Price's weaknesses (phrased, of course, with the utmost tact), Sharon has taken for a catalogue of his strengths (because they would be strengths in America). The first problem is that Price is "extremely devoted to his work," about which (the second problem) he is apparently "quite serious." The British work as hard as any people and take their work quite seriously, but work is normally not seen as something one should be devoted to or anything that is itself "serious," as in having consequence or inherent significance. To the British (and to most Europeans), work is merely the means to an end, the end being time with friends and family, time for recreation and sports, the chance to read and cultivate the arts, the opportunity for travel and leisure, the chance to improve the mind. In this scheme work itself is not important; it merely gives you the means to do what *is* important. Accordingly, people like Price who take work too seriously, what Americans would call a workaholic, do not impress the British.

Price is not only devoted to his work, he lets his devotion show. "He's enthusiastic," Miranda points out, "and gets quite worked up." It's bad enough to take work a tad too seriously, but it's even worse to be conspicuous about it. While everyone should be enthusiastic and energetic, of course, transparent enthusiasm and eagerness (getting worked up) come across to the British as showing off or self-promotion, both of which are very bad form. The British greatly admire people who can excel without obvious effort, almost casually, with plenty of time left over for a leisurely game of golf. If people have noticed Price's energy, then he's probably trying a bit too hard.

Enthusiasm bothers the British for another reason; it suggests that a person is on the verge of being carried away—by his or her emotions, naturally—and that the rational side is therefore no longer in control. As everyone knows, when people are in the grip of their emotions, anything can happen. In England, however, where manners and good form are paramount, only *certain* things are ever supposed to happen.

Another factor in play here is the vestigial British snob-
bery regarding work and especially business, what has been
called "the contempt of the squirearchy for useful knowledge" (Hill 1994, 75). To the British, work, particularly
the trades and manufacturing, is not altogether respectable. Traditionally, a gentleman didn't work at all if he
could help it—that's what made him a gentleman—and if
he couldn't help it, then he tossed work off with as little
effort and as much dispatch as possible, thereby saving his
energy (and his enthusiasm) for higher callings. "Being in
trade," one observer has noted,

> was always slightly low-status in the "best" com-
> pany in ninetenth century Britain.... Anti-indus-
> trial landed values overlaid British business life with
> a pretense that "we're not really in this for the
> money." British businessmen were...and still are
> at pains to appear to be gentlemen meeting around
> a kind of hobby, and then going away to their place
> in the country and leading gentlemen lives.
> (Djursaa 1994, 144–45)

Work does generate income, of course, which is nothing
to sneer at, but the making of money is likewise not something a true gentleman ever speaks of or worries about.

This traditional, somewhat disdainful view of work and
business has been called the cult of the amateur, and it has
come in for much analysis and soul-searching in recent
years. It has been blamed for everything from the British
lack of aggressiveness to their dismissive attitude toward
marketing and public relations to their reluctance to in-
novate—in short, for Britain's long and steady economic
decline. Even as basic a business concept as competition
has had its detractors in England. One of the reasons con-

sumer goods cost so much there compared with America and the rest of Europe—including products manufactured in England, such as Land Rover's Discovery model made in Birmingham, which costs $46,000 in the UK and $31,000 in Holland—is traditional business reluctance to compete on price. "There has been a culture here of non-competition," a British consumer advocate recently observed. "That whole American thing of beating the other store on price—that was considered unseemly" (Reid 1999, A19).

Sharon comes from a culture with very nearly the opposite attitudes toward work and business. Americans never struggled with quasi-aristocratic hangups about work or business, the notion that it's not suitable for a gentleman or that one should hold one's nose whilst engaged in buying and selling. It is, rather, a culture where work is celebrated and where being in business is entirely respectable. Not surprisingly, the qualities associated with hard work and dedication to one's job, the qualities Sharon has observed in Price, are virtues in her culture and therefore reasons for Price to at least be considered for the director position.

From the beginning, work was never anything to be ashamed of in America. Well, *almost* from the beginning, if one excludes the experiences of Jamestown and Plymouth, which were the very beginning of the British colonial era. In his book *American Beliefs*, John McElroy points out that those two early settlements nearly collapsed because of the misguided insistence of upper-class settlers that gentlemen did not do manual labor. "The culture of England," he points out, "where land was owned by gentlemen and worked by peasants for the benefit of the owners, was a threat to survival in the Virginia wilderness" (1999, 42) because unless everyone worked, there would not be

enough land cleared and enough food grown to provide
for both laborers and owners.

> Because agricultural work demands continual
> manual labor and because the vast majority of work-
> ers in early America were engaged in agriculture,
> manual work of all kinds assumed a cultural respect-
> ability it did not have in the aristocratic culture of
> Europe, where almost all the land was owned by a
> few persons who considered themselves socially and
> morally superior to those who rented and worked
> their lands....
>
> Landowners in colonial America and later peri-
> ods of American history worked side by side in the
> fields with their hired help and ate with them at
> the same table when they came into the house for
> meals. European travelers to America often re-
> marked on this behavior, which astonished them
> in being so different from the sharp class distinc-
> tion in Europe between those who got their hands
> dirty and those who did not. (48)

Since there was never a class that didn't work in America,
there was never anyone to look down on work from on
high. Moreover, the Puritan ethic taught that work was
inherently good, even redemptive.

For these reasons, there has always been an emphasis
on achievement in America, and in particular on judging
people (and oneself) according to achievements. Social
status and personal prestige, the esteem and regard of others, depend largely on what one has accomplished in life—
on what one has *done* with one's life, as Americans often
say—not on family name, education, or social class. It is
only natural, then, that work, which is the primary means

to achievement, would be taken very seriously. Nor should it be surprising that being enthusiastic and energetic about one's work, what Americans call being driven, is regarded as a positive quality. Indeed, Americans don't entirely trust people who are too disengaged, who don't take work seriously enough. They want to see the passion.

4. Rewrite

This dialogue goes by so fast it's hard to imagine culture had a chance to get a word in edgewise, but it did—twice, in fact—with the result that each speaker has an entirely different understanding of what has just transpired. In a nutshell, American directness has just met British indirectness, and they're not a very handsome couple.

As a rule, the British prefer to suggest and imply anything that might have a whiff of unpleasantness about it, such as criticism or negative feedback—anything, in short, that could lead to a dreaded "scene." Criticism will often be disguised, dressed up in something quite different from the way it appears, different, that is, to more direct Americans but not to other British. This dialogue features two such disguises. The first is Hugh's question: "Are you pleased with it?" This is a common ploy for indirect communicators, to toss a difficult question, difficult in the sense that the answer is negative, back at the questioner rather than answering it and thereby upsetting or disappointing you. This refusal to answer signals the other person (though not Carol) that the real answer, if it were actually given, would be awkward and is therefore being sidestepped altogether. This is still an answer, of course, to the British; it just happens to come in the form of a question.

The British know how this game is played, but Carol

doesn't. She assumes a question is a question, not a disguised answer, and responds accordingly ("Quite"). Hugh is now obliged to try another approach here, the second disguise, which is to avoid answering Carol's second question altogether ("Up to you, really"). Once again, if Carol were British she would realize that when another person has understood your question and declines to answer it, that's normally because the answer is going to be disappointing and the speaker would prefer not to reply. After all, if Hugh was going to agree with Carol or say something that would please her, why would he try to dodge her question? You don't need to sidestep giving good news, only bad; in other words, when the British avoid a question there's almost always a good reason.

Why does Carol miss all this? Why doesn't she read into Hugh's replies the meanings he intends? Part of the explanation is that Americans are more direct than the British. Accustomed to saying what they think and meaning what they say, Americans aren't good at reading between the lines when other people speak or at looking for the message in what is not said. Americans don't hear what is not said, and they tend to say what they mean, so it's not necessary to look elsewhere. A question is a question, in other words, not an answer in disguise, and an unanswered question is simply a question without an answer, not some kind of dodge. By and large, people are only able to recognize communication techniques they use themselves, and since Americans aren't used to disguising their answers, they don't recognize disguised answers when they hear them. It doesn't occur to them that such things might be answers to questions because they would never be in their culture.

How to account for British indirectness (as Americans

see it)? Part of the explanation surely lies in the legacy of feudalism. In highly stratified societies, one's well-being depended in large part on the continued goodwill and sufferance of one's betters. In such circumstances, people quickly learn to be circumspect in their speech, to say what they think other people want to hear, and (as in the dialogue) to find ways to avoid saying what other people don't want to hear. If curbing your tongue keeps a roof over your head and mutton in the stew pot, then you learn to be indirect.

For their part, Americans associate plain speaking with liberty; not being afraid to say what you think is perhaps the ultimate expression of individual freedom. It is, moreover, a symbol of equality, that no one is beholden or subservient to anyone else. "Rank of birth is not recognized," an early German visitor to America wrote, and "is resisted with a total force.... People think, act, and speak here precisely as it prompts them" (Degler 1984, 106). American directness may also be related to the fact that there was so much opportunity in the New World. What did it matter if you spoke your mind and caused offense? You could always go to a new place and start your life over.

Yet another cause of American directness may be the heterogeneous nature of the culture. As noted earlier, England's policy of open immigration made the American colonies a cornucopia of nationalities, all living and working cheek by jowl. Unlike people from more homogeneous countries, where everyone shares the same long national experience and the values and beliefs shaped thereby, people from more diverse societies have much less in common, much less that they intuitively know and understand about each other. The homogeneous types need not be explicit when they communicate, trusting the other party to fill in (from that shared understanding) what has been left unsaid (or, more accurately, what has not been deemed *necessary* to say). People from culturally mixed societies, however, can't trust their listeners to intuit their meaning—to say some of what they mean, for example, and expect listeners to correctly supply the rest. In such cultures, whatever is left unsaid is left uncommunicated.

It should be noted, in closing, that while Americans often find the British indirect, this is an entirely subjective judgment. The British find each other direct enough, even blunt in some cases, and while they can certainly be indirect according to their own standards, true British indirectness would no doubt go unremarked by the average Yank. By the same token, Americans have their version of indirect and subtle, though it wouldn't strike the British that way; real American directness would probably empty most British drawing rooms.

5. Dropping By

"They're so forward," a British woman says of Americans in Bill Bryson's delightful book, *Notes from a Small Island*:

> You've only to chat with a stranger for five minutes and they think you've become *friends*. I had some man in Encino—a retired postal worker or some such thing—asking my address and promising to call *round* next time he's in England. Can you imagine it? I'd never met the man in my life. (1995, 258)

Like most Europeans, the British are a much more private and formal people than their American cousins are, especially with regard to their family life. While Americans

have an easy, casual way with each other, even with relative strangers, the British instinct is to keep one's distance
when possible. Among the British, access to another person is granted rather than presumed, whether it's access to
one's interior life, to what a person is thinking or feeling,
or to one's exterior life, such as one's home. In such a world,
dropping by someone's home unannounced is practically
tantamount to breaking and entering and would, in all
probability, be met with a similar kind of shock. (Readers
should note that in this dialogue it is the British man,
Adrian, and his family who have moved into the neighborhood where the expat American lives.)

In the dialogue Adrian may feel he has been ambushed
by Debbie, a complete stranger, who introduces herself and
starts up a conversation. While the British can certainly
handle such informality, and even indulge in it themselves
on occasion, they tend to be wary of imposing themselves
on a stranger—what if that person wanted to be left
alone?—and normally wait until they are introduced by a
third party. Be that as it may, all goes relatively well in the
conversation until Debbie starts zeroing in on Adrian's
home and, by implication, his family and private life, where
Adrian feels compelled to draw the line. It's one thing to
strike up conversations with strangers, but it's another to
invite them in for tea—or unpacking boxes. And it's unthinkable that they would just drop in unannounced.
Adrian's remark about his telephone is an extremely polite—and very direct—warning to Debbie *not* to drop by
without calling (the British say "ringing up") ahead of time.
In that way when Debbie and company do come to visit,
Adrian and his family will have had time to prepare themselves and that part of their home that is available for public consumption. They will be dressed in the clothes they

want strangers to see them in, doing whatever it is they don't mind strangers seeing them doing, and taking tea in the sitting room arranged the way they want strangers to see it. As for unpacking boxes, boxes contain the family's belongings. Belongings tell the story of a person's life; and that story is for close friends and family.

Debbie would be shocked, horrified even, to learn of the panic she has unleashed in Adrian's world. She was only trying to be friendly. Adrian is the new man in the office, after all, and probably doesn't know many people, so she wants to put him at ease and make him feel at home. As for dropping by his house, it would almost be rude not to if you're in the neighborhood, especially if you're walking right by! It doesn't matter how you're dressed or what state the house or yard is in; we all know people are more casual when they're at home. And unpacking boxes would be a pleasant way to get to know Adrian and his family better. Because of her American mindset, Debbie takes no notice of Adrian's remark about the telephone and likewise misses the fact that he never does give her his street number.

Needless to say, American informality often catches Europeans off guard. "While Europeans [think] of their houses as castles or sanctuaries," Richard Pells has noted, "surrounded by gates, hedges, or high walls…, Americans [live] behind picture windows, their domestic arrangements 'exposed to the gaze of every passer-by,' implying they have nothing to hide from the outside world" (1997, 171).

"Old world distinctions between 'private' and 'public' aspects of life tended to lose meaning [in America]," Daniel Boorstin observes.

> "Home," in England an intimate and emotion-laden word, in America became almost inter-

changeable with "house." Here was both less privacy and more publicity. Americans lived in a new realm of uncertain boundaries, in an affable, communal world which, strictly speaking, was neither public nor private: a world of first names, open doors, front porches, and front lawns.... In this new limbo, family life lost much of its old privacy. Casual acquaintances soon seemed members of the family. (1965, 44)

In the end, because of Debbie and Adrian's entirely different views of the proper way to treat strangers or new acquaintances, she may come across to him as pushy and forward, and Adrian may strike her as distant and unfriendly. These are, in fact, among the most common charges traded by these two cultures.

The British (and European) attitude toward privacy is not hard to explain. On a practical level, privacy, like anything that is scarce, is the more highly prized for being so hard to come by. Compared with Americans, Europeans in general live on top of each other—and the British in particular are packed in like kippered herrings. Martin Gannon has pointed out that whereas the population density on the continent is 146 people per square kilometer, in England it's 235. England is half the size of California and home to twice as many people. "Because physical distance [from other people] isn't possible," Gannon notes, "the only available protection of personal space is psychological distance" (1994, 26). And in those places where physical distance is possible, inside one's home, for example, and behind one's hedgerows, it is practically insisted upon.

"Most Britons have at least one thing in common," Gannon continues, a respect and a strong desire for privacy. This sentiment is so strong that they often appear to others as distant and aloof.... The phrase "We like to keep ourselves to ourselves" is particularly British. Glyn notes that even in the case of child care, baby sitters need to be hired because relatives will generally not help or interfere.

A good neighbor is one who is friendly at a distance—who does not intrude. One should always phone ahead before visiting a British home. Dropping in unannounced would generally be unwelcome. Also, frequent social telephone calls tend to be regarded as an intrusion. (26, 27)

While Americans and the British both tend to live in cities, Americans don't usually have to live on top of each other unless they want to. Whereas the British cluster in villages tucked ever more tightly between large open agricultural areas, Americans build more or less where it pleases them. Many people live in housing developments, of course, but even there the lots tend to be much larger than in England, and most people have their own "detached" house (as compared with the British "semidetached" home, which is a single structure with two separate entrances and living quarters). As Crèvecoeur observed of the typical immigrant to America, "He does not find, as in Europe, a crowded society, where every place is over-stocked; he does not feel that perpetual collision of parties..., that contention which oversets so many" (Boorstin 1958, 188). Where privacy is a matter of course, people tend to be more casual about it.

6. Moving Up

Discussions of the role of class in British society are cultural minefields that any outsider enters at great peril. The British themselves are greatly conflicted on the subject; while everyone more or less agrees that class matters less than it once did, there is very little agreement on just how much it still influences British behavior. For every illustration one can offer of class in action, such as this dialogue, a very similar illustration can be found that refutes the first. More than most cultural phenomena, the role of class depends very much on context. Paul Gibbs, the author of *Doing Business in the European Community*, probably speaks for most of the British when he writes,

> It would be wrong, particularly in the City of London, to assume that ability, drive and ambition have yet overtaken the traditional social advantages of belonging to the "right family" (old money), having a public school education (fee paying), and going to the right university, namely Oxford or Cambridge. (1992, 206)

One thing is certain, though: however much the British may disagree among themselves on the place class occupies in their society, to Americans, with little direct experience of the phenomenon, there are signs of class wherever you turn (and that's allowing for the fact that Americans don't even see most of the signs of class in England). In his book *Living and Working Abroad: London*, Orin Hargraves, an American who lived and worked several years in that city, pulls no punches when it comes to the subject. "Class," he writes,

> is the index that Britons use to establish how they

fit in, and how others fit into their society. In other
words, it is a significant component of most British people's identity. Despite protests to the contrary, and the stated intention of the government
to create a classless society, the class system is still
very much alive. (1997, 48)

The concept of class runs straight through Arthur's re-
sponses, for example, whereas every line the American,
Todd, speaks betrays his ignorance of the subject or, more
accurately, reveals key differences between American and
British attitudes toward class. Indeed, if Todd understood
more about the subject, this conversation would never have
gotten off the ground, for he would not assume that someone of the working class, like Arthur, would be inclined to
make the leap to management—hence, to the middle class.
While Arthur certainly could make the leap in today's
England, changing class more often requires the passage
of one or more generations. Regardless of whether or not
Arthur *could* make the move, the bigger question is whether
he would want to, which he answers quite unequivocally
when he balks at the prospect, saying "I don't know any of
those people." Changing social classes, especially going
from the working to the middle class, is still widely regarded in England as a kind of betrayal, of trying to be
something you're not, and it often leaves class jumpers in
a kind of no-man's-land, not really accepted by the class
they aspire to join and no longer welcome in the one they
are perceived to have turned their back on. It may be this
very prospect that gives Arthur pause. Or it may be a related reason, the fact that England, as Ian Buruma points
out, is "the only western European country that still [has]
a true working class, with its own class traditions and cul-

ture, in which it [takes] pride" (1998, 15). Be that as it may, Arthur's view actually should have been clear to Todd even before this, from Arthur's first line ("I wonder who they'll select"), that he has never imagined himself a manager and wouldn't be interested in a vacancy.

Todd's final line reveals his unfamiliarity with another aspect of the class system, the fact that people from different classes don't typically become friends. All other things being equal—and they often are not—people tend to have friends from their own social background. Thus, Todd's assumption that Arthur would know the people in management because he has been with the company for several years is probably invalid. Arthur no doubt has friends among the people in his shop—though it is true that on the whole Europeans socialize less with co-workers than Americans do—but probably not in management; they aren't his "type."

If all this makes Todd sound particularly obtuse (which may be how he comes across to Arthur), it's certainly not meant to. He misses the cues in the dialogue not because he's dim-witted but because he views the whole question of moving up from an American perspective. By and large, the class system never caught on in America, and consequently people tend not to think in terms of class. Egalitarianism, after all, the notion that everyone is *inherently* equal, is one of the bedrock values of American culture. America was the great meritocracy (as opposed to an aristocracy), a country where people got ahead (or did not) on the basis of ambition and hard work and not because of birth or social status. Many of the people who settled America came expressly to escape a world of inherited rank and privilege and, not surprisingly, founded a culture where rank and privilege had to be earned through one's own efforts. While some segments of American society might argue that this is more the ideal than the reality, it is certainly more real in the United States than in England. For Todd, then, the only thing that could be keeping Arthur from moving up would have to be either a lack of ambition or, perhaps, no interest in being a manager. Since Arthur doesn't seem to lack for ambition, Todd assumes he might be interested in a management job and therefore informs him of the vacancy.

It's entirely possible, incidentally, that the reason Arthur doesn't want to move up has nothing to do with class and everything to do with Arthur: that he likes the hours he works, for example, or doesn't like the new people he would be working with. Or he may be thinking of changing companies. Culture is always a possible but never the only reason behind another person's behavior; but in dealing with the British, though, Americans (and others) would be wise to keep class in mind in virtually any kind of interaction.

7. All the Stops

For the British, there is such a thing as giving up gracefully, admitting defeat, and moving on. You must always try your best, of course, using every arrow in your quiver, but there comes a time when persistence is unbecoming, not to mention arrogant. There are limits, after all, to what one can do and to what one can be expected to do in any given situation, and to carry on past those limits is simply bad form. Knowing when to give up and being able to give up with style are signs of maturity. This is not considered failure, by the way—failure is stopping before you have made your best effort—but merely resignation, recognizing that's the way things are and acting accordingly.

Amanda demonstrates this attitude clearly in several places in the dialogue and assumes that Tom is agreeing with her. Only at the end does she realize he does not. When she points out they've tried everything they can think of, this is her way of saying that while she too wants to continue until they have exhausted all the possibilities, she *does* want to stop when they have. Since Tom can't think of any stone that hasn't been turned here, Amanda assumes he is also ready to stop and then offers what she clearly intends as words of comfort: "We did our best," meaning that nothing more could realistically be expected. Then she adds her strongest point, that nobody else has ever managed this particular trick either. She's taken aback, and probably offended, when Tom replies that he's not a quitter. She doesn't consider either of them a quitter because she doesn't regard what they're doing to be quitting.

So why does Tom misread her so completely? The answer lies in the fact that Americans have a very different attitude toward limits, and Tom, therefore, has a very different take on the situation in the dialogue. For Tom the only limits are those one sets oneself; limits don't exist in nature, in other words, they exist only inside the person. Accordingly, there's no tradition of recognizing that's just how things are and resigning oneself to the facts. For people like Tom, however things *may* be, they can always be changed. All problems have solutions if you work on them long enough. Needless to say, giving in, with or without style, doesn't readily fit into the picture. Since there are no *real* limits, giving up simply means yielding to your own self-imposed lack of will or resolve. You could go on, in other words, but you've simply decided not to.

Tom doesn't see any handwriting on the wall, to use Amanda's phrase; the only writing on walls in his universe is whatever he scratches there himself. One is reminded of the scene in *Lawrence of Arabia* when Lawrence's Bedouin friend Ali tells him he can do nothing about a certain turn of events because these things "are written." Lawrence replies that "nothing is written" except what's "in here" and taps the side of his head. Tom is not impressed, as Amanda seems to be, that they have tried everything they can think of. That may be a standard for some people, but to Tom it just means they have to think harder. Nor is he comforted when she says they've done their best. Clearly they haven't or they would have cracked this problem. Nor is her remark that no one has ever done this before quite the balm Amanda thinks it is; telling someone like Tom that better people than he have failed to solve this problem is nothing less than a call to action.

This is all part of the fabled "can-do" attitude of Americans, the notion that anything that can be conceived of can always be tried, and anything that can be tried can ultimately be achieved. This is especially true of things that have never been done before or that people generally believe cannot be done; such tasks pose an almost irresistible challenge to Americans. The typical American response to any suggestion, then, no matter how far-fetched, is "Let's try it." And once any scheme is set in motion, Americans are convinced that one way or another it can be accomplished. The British, it must be said, have almost the opposite reaction to any suggestion that is the least bit out of the ordinary or unusual; they are wary and doubtful. Even if such a thing could be done, it probably shouldn't be. After all, if something has never been attempted before, then there's probably a very good reason. If America is a can-do culture, then England is a "mustn't do" one.

What accounts for these different notions of limits and

of what is and is not possible in life? The answer lies in part with a concept known as the locus of control, which deals with where people believe the responsibility lies for what happens in life. Americans believe the locus of control is internal, inside the person, and that what happens is therefore largely up to the individual. "The American born descendants of the immigrants [had] several non-European attitudes," John McElroy has written, including the core belief "that the past does not determine the future but that the actions of men can shape the future to a desired end" (1999, 67–68). Americans are not great believers in fate or luck, in other words, in the power of external events to shape their lives. Rather, they believe people make their own luck and shape their own destiny. This was certainly the lesson of their early experience in the New World, and nothing in their history since that time has caused them to think otherwise. Indeed, as far as limits are concerned, the American story is all about rejecting and transcending limits, pushing the frontier across the country and into the Pacific Ocean—and then going to the moon.

Another factor here is the sheer size of the country and the abundance of its resources, which made it virtually impossible for any notion of limits to get a foothold in the American character. One only had to look around to see there was no such thing as limits. "Unlimited space was not just a physical attribute of the American continent," Richard Pells has observed,

> it was...a key to the American psyche. Here the disparities between the United States and Europe were obvious. In small countries like Britain, Switzerland, or Italy, those who lived there noted, spatial restric-

tions led to…a sense of limited possibilities. In America, Harold Laski asserted, the horizons were infinite and so too were the opportunities. There were few obstacles to economic or social ascent. In Laski's view, "the element of spaciousness in American life" resulted in a dynamism that was the opposite of European "rigidity." (1997, 169)

For the British, their national experience has taught them that you can't always prevail and that there will be reverses in life (the loss of empire) as well as advances. It has taught them, in other words, that to some extent the locus of control is external, that there are certain givens in life, certain circumstances over which we have no control and which must therefore be accepted. This doesn't mean the British are a passive people, bowing to the inevitable and lamenting the loss of empire (though it must be said they do adopt this pose on occasion); it means, rather, that they are an eminently practical people, given to cold, objective analysis and not afraid to cut their losses. They will try their best—they're not slackers—but they believe that there comes a point beyond which trying is no longer a virtue.

The aristocratic tradition is also no doubt responsible in part for the British habit of resignation. Born into a world where their future was more or less determined from birth, where there was little chance of advancing beyond their station, people didn't spend their lives bemoaning lost opportunities. Instead, they made the best of their lot, enjoying, if they were lucky, the occasional modest improvement and minor amelioration. In such a world, limits were as natural as the air one breathed. "When the citizens of a community are classed according to rank, profession or birth," Alexis de Tocqueville wrote,

> and when all men are constrained to follow the career which chance has opened before them, everyone thinks that the utmost limits of human power are to be discerned in proximity to himself, and no one seeks any longer to resist the inevitable law of his destiny. Not, indeed, that an aristocratic people absolutely deny man's faculty of self-improvement, but they do not hold it to be indefinite; they can conceive amelioration, but not change; they imagine that the future condition of society may be better, but not essentially different; and whilst they admit that humanity has made progress, and may still have some to make, they assign to it beforehand certain impassable limits. (1984, 159)

In the end the real cultural difference between Tom and Amanda may not be so much that Tom is likely to carry on long after Amanda has thrown in the towel, but in how each of them feels at the moment of capitulation. Amanda is at peace, having done all that could reasonably be expected, while Tom has a nagging doubt that he should have tried harder. If Tom comes across as naive and unrealistic in Amanda's mind, then she no doubt comes across as defeatist to him.

8. Calling a Cab

Stoicism comes very close to being the British national virtue. It's the notion behind the stiff upper lip, after all, the British national pose, and is likewise at the heart of what is perhaps the greatest of all British preoccupations:

cheerfully doing without. Cold showers, dull food, no central heating, the National Health Service—the British are
great fans of adversity. The idea seems to be that since by
and large life is a struggle, you have to be tough to survive.
Nice things may happen from time to time, of course, and
you can enjoy them when they do, but don't be fooled:
they aren't the norm and they won't last. As the British
are fond of reminding their children, you are not put on
this earth to enjoy yourself.

Not surprisingly, the British are great believers in self-
denial and self-restraint. Holding back builds character and
makes you strong, and it suggests you have mastered that
other great British virtue: control over your emotions. In
such a scheme, nearly all pleasures are guilty ones, and
self-indulgence is for the very weak. If you must indulge
yourself, then be sure to let on that you know it's bad for
you and that you won't be making a habit of it. "The British actually like their pleasures small," Bill Bryson writes.

> That is why so many of their treats—tea cakes,
> scones, crumpets, rock cakes, rich tea biscuits, fruit
> Shrewsburys—are so cautiously flavorful.... Offer
> them something genuinely tempting—a slice of
> gateau or a choice of chocolates from a box—and
> they will nearly always hesitate and begin to worry
> that it's unwarranted and excessive, as if any plea-
> sure beyond a very modest threshold is vaguely
> unseemly.
> "Oh, I shouldn't really," they say.
> "Oh, go on," you prod encouragingly.
> "Well, just a small one then," they say and
> dartingly take a small one, and then look as if they
> have just done something terribly devilish. (1995,
> 79)

You can have your guilty pleasures, in other words, just make sure you really do feel guilty.

Naturally, anyone who expects life to be a struggle, like Rowan in the dialogue, isn't surprised when it is— and certainly doesn't expect recognition or sympathy merely for coping. Coping is a given. Rowan cheerfully accepts that there will be days like this, times when you will have to work late and be inconvenienced; he expects to have to make personal sacrifices from time to time and sees nothing remarkable about it. It's all part of being a grown-up. He doesn't understand, therefore, when Ann says the two of them have performed "above and beyond the call of duty." For Rowan, duty simply means getting the job done, and if that's all these two have accomplished, then they certainly haven't done anything *more* than their duty. Hence his response, "All in a day's work."

Ann sees things rather differently, in large part because she doesn't regard life as a struggle and notices, therefore, whenever it becomes one. Americans have been accused of a multitude of sins, but stoicism is not one of them. The United States is the country where more is better, the country that perfected instant gratification and that has come closer than any other to figuring out how to have your cake and eat it, too. *Self* and *denial* aren't words ever put next to each other in the U.S. and ditto for *guilty* and *pleasure*.

For Ann, then, the threshold for personal sacrifice and inconvenience—what constitutes going beyond the call of duty—is rather lower than it is for Rowan. Working until 8:30, for example, more than meets the test and is certainly not "all in a day's work." It is, rather, in a long day's work. Rowan, who is somewhat taken aback here, merely adds that even if such a thing *is* remarkable, at least it "doesn't happen that often." Things now go from bad to worse with Ann's revelation that she has ordered a cab (to take them home) and that she would like to charge the expense to the company. For Rowan, who has yet to see the inconvenience in this picture, the cab is an unnecessary extravagance—and charging it to the company is clearly over the top. For Ann, meanwhile, the cab is simply a well-earned reward for which a grateful employer will happily pay. Is it any surprise that the British sometimes find Americans soft and spoiled or that Americans think the British actually enjoy suffering?

Luigi Barzini thinks stoicism is the inevitable by-product of the harsh conditions and hard lives that made up the daily lot of the British for centuries. It is, he says, the quality

> of sailors on sailing ships who face raging seas and hurricanes or wait weeks for the windless calm to end; [of] farmers on inhospitable land, resigned to the unpredictable weather; [of] fishermen in the stormy and fog-bound seas of the North; [of] lonely shepherds on deserted moors.... Surely it was their hard life that taught the British to be brave, resourceful, far-seeing, self-controlled, or to act as if they were. In one word, they are stoics.

> Most of them were stoics to begin with long ago.... Later most of them still behaved like stoics, whether they were or not, because that was the way to be and it was inconceivable to be anything else. (1983, 61–62)

By and large, living conditions in America were not as harsh as those in England, except perhaps in New England, where, not surprisingly, there is still a deep stoic tradition.

There was an abundance of resources and opportunity, which meant that while life *could* be a struggle, it certainly didn't have to be. Indeed, the whole point in the New World was that life didn't *have* to be anything; it was whatever you made of it. You didn't have to deny yourself things, in other words, or suffer in silence, and to this day, Americans find little nobility in stoicism; it's just a convenient excuse for people who have given up.

9. Office Mates

Compared with Americans, the British are a reserved and guarded people. They have an almost instinctive protectiveness of their inner thoughts and feelings and are likewise extremely careful not to intrude uninvited upon the private lives of others. Their instinct is to grant others plenty of emotional and psychological distance, and they expect to be granted the same in return. "British reserve and an inbred awkwardness with personal contact," John Mole has written, "creates arm's length relationship[s] in which both sides are on their guard" (1995, 95). The safest course with the British, therefore, is to err on the side of revealing too little of yourself, of holding back, than of revealing too much, which the British might find embarrassing. Under the circumstances, the pace at which friendships develop among the British is considerably slower than among Americans. Thus, even if Roger does share an office with the troubled Blanchard, eight months would hardly be enough time for Blanchard to feel comfortable opening up about personal problems.

So why does Roger think it would be enough time? And why does he miss all the other cues in the dialogue (see the analysis below) about the nature of interpersonal relationships in England? In brief, because Roger is an American, and people from the United States see these things rather differently. Americans are somewhat notorious for how quickly and readily they open themselves up to others, granting considerable access at the drop of a hat. You can easily get an American's life story in a short plane trip or over coffee at the lunch counter, often with intimate details. Self-revelation is practically a norm in the U.S. and is not considered especially intrusive or an invasion of privacy. Indeed, people who aren't particularly forthcoming or revealing about themselves, who "hold back" (as Americans sometimes say), come across as closed and unfriendly. They wonder why someone would be guarded and whether they can trust such a person, or if he or she might have something to hide. Why else would someone be so reserved? "When I make new acquaintances," a Polish professor writes of his experiences in America,

> I discover that I am learning many intimate details of the personal lives of the people I have just met. I find myself a bit embarrassed, but I doubt that they are. They become my friends so quickly, and as quickly they begin to share their problems with me.... In America, when one meets someone, he or she immediately becomes a friend. (DeVita and Armstrong 1993, 23)

For Roger, then, eight months would be more than enough time to become close to another person, especially an office mate, which is why he's so sure Blanchard's problems aren't marital, or he would have said something. What Roger really means, of course, is that *another American* might have shared a confidence of this sort after eight months as office mates, and he just assumes Blanchard would have too.

If Roger had been listening closely to Julia, he would have heard that his assumptions were wrong from the beginning. When he says she must know Blanchard after all the time they've worked together, he's assuming that people make friends with their fellow workers, which is common in America but less so in Europe. Julia's answer ("We've been colleagues for a year, if that's what you mean") is intended to inform Roger (1) that she and Blanchard are not friends (that's why she's chosen the word *colleague*) and (2) that even if they were inclined to become friends, a year is hardly long enough for that to happen. If there is any lingering doubt about how well Julia knows Blanchard, it is dispelled in her next line, "It must be something personal," meaning these two do not in fact share confidences. For his part, Roger thinks Julia is merely categorizing the nature of Blanchard's problem, personal as opposed to professional, not that she is describing the nature of their relationship, and he responds accordingly. In the end, Julia has to be wondering why Roger thinks co-workers would be so intimate with each other, and Roger is no doubt puzzled by how closed and protective the British are about their private lives.

Most observers of Americans feel it's the great mobility of their society that makes them so quick to open up. People move easily and frequently—the average American gets a new mortgage every seven years, and over half of all Americans live more than fifty miles from where they grew up—which means that if friendships don't develop quickly, they don't develop at all. "People in transition and upstart communities," Daniel Boorstin notes, "had to become accustomed to live and eat and talk in the presence of those they knew only casually" (1965, 147). The absence of a class system may also be a factor here; where

people do not have to worry about transgressing class bar-
riers, there's little risk in approaching others and being
informal.

The British, as noted previously, are much less mobile.
"Britons tend not to move too far away from their family
homes," Martin Gannon has written.

> They are not inclined to make changes simply for
> the sake of change; they prefer to stick with famil-
> iar and comfortable surroundings. Moving across
> town is not treated lightly, and one would need a
> good reason to move to another part of the coun-
> try. Lack of work is often not considered to be a
> strong enough motivator to move away from one's
> home and roots. (1994, 31)

The lack of mobility can also be explained by the fact
that people have traditionally not changed jobs very often
and that even when they do so, they often do not change
residences. The latter is because of the relative smallness
of the country (compared with America) and the excel-
lent rail system, which together mean that in much of England, and especially the south, the average person lives
within commuting distance of a third or more of the rest
of the country. Hence, the British can still be quite profes-
sionally mobile and never have to leave their town or village. Since friendships may very well be for life, therefore,
there is no particular urgency about them nor any reason
they can't develop at a more gradual pace. It may also be
the case that the sensitivities of the class system dictated a
more cautious approach to befriending others; one would
not want to make the mistake of opening oneself up to
people who turned out to be below or above one's station.

10. Well Done

This dialogue deals with the notion of taking credit for one's achievements and the related subject of having attention drawn to oneself. On the whole, the British are a self-deprecating, self-effacing lot for whom the correct response to any kind of praise or recognition is modesty and humility. They are somewhat uncomfortable with recognition, in other words, and generally prefer a low personal profile.

As is so often the case with the British, this is as much a matter of appearances as of reality. The British are as proud of a job well done as anyone, but it's decidedly bad form to *appear* proud. They expect and appreciate praise when it is deserved, but they know better than to *act* as if it's deserved. They also feel, as illustrated in the dialogue, that however well one may have performed, the job could always have been done better. It's simply good manners, therefore, to acknowledge room for improvement; hence, Martin's automatic and entirely ritual disclaimer ("I wish we'd had more time") when Tom praises him.

Alas, Tom now takes Martin's formulaic response literally, mistaking a ritual disclaimer for a real one, and insists that Martin accept the praise ("It really couldn't have been better"), thereby obliging poor Martin to deflect yet another compliment ("I wouldn't like to think so"). For an American like Tom, who sees no reason why a person wouldn't accept praise where it was deserved, Martin's determination to duck compliments is beginning to feel suspicious. Hence his next comment, "You mean you left something out?" Martin means nothing of the kind, of course ("Excuse me?"), and we're right back where we started.

It's all a matter of degree. Americans value humility, too, and even have their own version of self-effacement ("Oh, it was nothing"), but it is not a religion with them. They are more comfortable with recognition and with having attention drawn to themselves and their achievements. Indeed, they tend to hand out compliments indiscriminately (and quite insincerely as far as the British are concerned), as if they were candy bars, and they accept them almost as readily. While it's bad form to solicit or revel in praise or compliments, there's no need to run from them so long as they're earned. In fact to Americans, too much self-deprecation sounds phony and may even suggest a lack of self-confidence. In the end, it is the tenacity with which Martin refuses recognition that catches Tom off guard.

From the American point of view, incidentally, the British can appear stingy with praise and encouragement, causing the Americans they work with to think they are performing poorly or not regarded highly enough. And the British, meanwhile, tend to discount praise from Americans; it's so common as to have no real meaning.

The British instinct toward self-deprecation is probably more fallout from the stoicism syndrome. If life is a struggle where only the tough prevail, then shrugging off compliments is simply proof of your toughness. Life is *supposed* to be hard, after all, and we shouldn't expect that much of what we do will be appreciated; we do something because it's the right thing, not because it will be recognized or rewarded. In such a world, people who need compliments, or, more precisely, people who *appear* to need compliments (we all need them, even the British), will be seen as weak.

As noted earlier, the British are not, by and large, a

hopeful people; they don't expect good things to happen. Indeed, when they do, the British are suspicious; we may have gotten lucky this time, but we shouldn't be fooled. Self-satisfaction is an attitude the British almost never indulge in. Luigi Barzini has described how

> stoic were the sober newspaper comments on the brilliant, skillful, and daring Falklands war...a highly pragmatic operation undertaken in defense of international law and morality and surely not for gain. I will quote only one comment, Alexander Chancellor's in the *Spectator* after the victory. It began, "A little rejoicing is now in order, but only a little. We may rejoice that the Falklands war did not end in a bloodbath at Port Stanley.... We may rejoice at the performance of our armed forces who have conducted themselves with great skill and with as much humanity as is possible in war." It is clearly inconceivable for anybody not a Briton to write so soberly after such a brilliant and risky military performance. (1983, 63)

11. Buying Blind

This dialogue compares the British and American attitudes toward risk taking and its close cousin, failure. Americans are notorious for taking risks, often unnecessarily, seemingly for the sheer thrill of it, while the British find no inherent value—and a great deal of inherent bother—in risk taking. For them (and for most Europeans), trial and error, and especially error, are *at best* something to be avoided whenever possible, and when it is not possible, then something to be minimized at every turn. There is no upside to risk, in other words, nothing to be gained, and a good deal to be lost. That's why they call it "risk." Nor is there any honor or bravery in taking risks. It is, rather, the refuge of the ill informed, the unprepared, and the lazy. Risks can't always be avoided, of course, but they should be a last resort, what you are forced to do when your plan fails. But risk taking should never *be* your plan. If you were asked to sum up the difference between life in the Old World and the New, you could do worse than to start with this whole idea of risk.

The real risk in risk taking, of course—the *problem*—is the possibility of failure, and the British and Americans have very different attitudes toward failure. In a word, the British fear it and Americans do not, as we see in this dialogue featuring the irrepressible Karen and the wary Derek. From the beginning, Derek is troubled, as he signals with his first comment, that the sudden appearance of Symonds Plc on the market is "quite unexpected." What he means is that there hasn't been any time to absorb this information yet, to check with one's sources and find out what's behind this surprise development. There hasn't been time, in short, to know even what to think of this turn of events, much less to act on it.

For her part Karen isn't afraid of acting before thinking, especially if waiting means losing an opportunity ("There's going to be a lot of interest"). Derek isn't sure this *is* an opportunity, of course, and isn't about to act until he knows. While his next remark ("I've heard it could sell in less than a month") seems to reassure Karen that they're both on the same page, what he actually means is that since a month isn't enough time to thoroughly investigate Symonds Plc, bidding would be risky. Any doubt about where Derek stands on the issue is cleared up in his next remark, that bidding on Symonds would be "buying blind," that is, buying without careful study, something that's just not done, at least not by cautious British companies. But Karen misses this too and proceeds to astound Derek with her statement that there isn't much time to get a bid together. Of course there won't be a bid except, apparently, from some risk-happy Americans.

This is not to say the British never take risks but only that they do so with great reluctance, either after carefully weighing the pros and cons or when there is simply no alternative. If the choice is between not acting and taking a risk, the British will generally choose the former. If the choice, however, is between certain disaster and taking a risk, then they will, against their better judgment, choose the risk. In the example in the dialogue, the British would be asking themselves not "Should we take a chance on Symonds?" but "Why didn't we know about this sooner?"

What accounts for British caution? Part of the explanation is the belief that risk taking isn't really necessary, that most outcomes can be known ahead of time because there's always a precedent for whatever one is doing, or one simply takes the time to think things through. This is a common attitude in older cultures that, unlike the United States, aren't making things up as they go along. If you live in a culture where people believe, rightly or wrongly, that they've seen it all before, then there's no need to take chances, to try things and see what happens. If you're acting responsibly, you should *know* what's going to happen. In this context, risk taking is simply sheer self-indulgence.

Another, equally important factor here is the relative lack of opportunity in Europe. Europeans don't have the tradition of starting over, of endless second chances; there's no frontier, no American west you can always decamp to

and begin again. You find a niche somewhere, after considerable effort and with the help of everyone you know,
you make it as secure as you can, and you consider yourself
a success. Risk, with its ever-present possibility of failure,
doesn't fit into this picture. In America, failure is just a
way station on the road to success; in Europe, it's very often the end of the line.

"The European becomes tired at the very idea of risk,"
Stuart Miller has observed.

> He wants security. He gets no big thrill from free-
> dom, opportunity, energy, and change, the way
> [Americans] do. Or, if he does, often he thinks of
> immigrating to the United States. As an Ameri-
> can, I find it shocking, for example, that 70 per-
> cent of the generation of Italy's famous economic
> boom, the kids born between 1960 and 1965, have
> the following aspiration: they want to find a *posto
> fisso*, a permanent government job, the kind that
> cannot by law ever be cut from any budget, even if
> society doesn't need it anymore.
>
> People may not always get much money for do-
> ing these jobs, but they want them. They want
> things quiet and steady and are willing to pay with
> boredom of almost infinite dimension. (1990, 61)

When it came to taking risks, Americans had no
choice. They were immigrants, after all, and immigrants
can't afford to be cautious. Just *getting* to the New World
was the first and perhaps greatest risk, crossing the notorious North Atlantic in a tiny boat and then stepping off
into a strange new world. It was not for everyone, of course,
and those for whom it was too daunting never entertained
the notion. "The discovery of the new world," George

Santayana has written,

> exercised a sort of selection among the inhabitants
> of Europe. The fortunate, the deeply rooted, and
> the lazy remained at home; the wilder instincts or
> dissatisfactions of others tempted them beyond the
> horizon. The American is accordingly the most
> adventurous, or the descendant of the most adven-
> turous, of Europeans. (in Degler 1984, 297)

Once they were on American shores, the immigrants
had to be willing to try things without knowing whether
they would work or what the consequences might be. The
country itself was nothing but an experiment, a commin-
gling of people from different countries and different classes
in a completely unfamiliar environment. Tradition, the
old ways, what one has always done—these were early casualties of life in the New World, replaced by trial and
error and a person's best guess. Nothing anyone did had a
precedent. "Important innovations," Daniel Boorstin
writes, "were made simply because Americans did not know
any better" (1965, 21)—or, if there was a precedent, then
it probably wasn't relevant in these conditions. Under the
circumstances, *to do anything at all* was to take a risk.

In such a culture, not surprisingly, the possibility of
failure—the real risk in risk taking—was something you
simply couldn't afford to worry about. After all, if merely
to act was to invite risk, then to fail could hardly be shameful. The fear of failure was also mitigated by another factor, the boundless opportunity that seemed to be available
in America. With so much land, so few people, so many
natural resources, and so few restraints of any kind—
whether legal, social, or psychological—the consequences
of failure were minor and short-lived. It was a country

where no matter what happened, you always got another chance, where opportunity was so rampant it simply wasn't possible to squander it. "The abundance of our material resources," Boorstin has observed, "has encouraged a wholesome unconcern for material things in themselves. We have been able to afford to experiment..." (1976, 54). In America, the only failure was to stop trying.

12. Vacancy

With indirect communicators, like the British, the message in any given conversational exchange may be contained in what is *not* said. This is particularly the case when what the speaker has to say is not going to be pleasant for the other party to hear. The problem, of course, is that direct communicators, like the American in this dialogue, don't "hear" what is not said, meaning that the listen-for-what-I-don't-say approach is not going to work.

Poor Don. He has left this conversation believing he might get the job in the finance department, or at least that he will be seriously considered, when in fact Simon has made it clear that Don is not in the running. In every statement Simon makes after his opening greeting, there is a conspicuous opportunity to give Don some encouragement, but Simon deliberately lets the opportunity pass in each case. When Don begins by saying he's heard about the vacancy, for example, surely Simon understands that Don must be thinking about applying. If he wanted Don to apply, he would say so at this point. But he says nothing. Can that really be accidental?

Then look at what happens next: Don says he's interested in applying for the job. And Simon still says nothing—or, rather, he says "Great" (he's not a boor, after all) and then says he's mulling over possible candidates—and doesn't mention Don as one of them. Another accident?

Now things get even more curious. Don declares he has an accounting background, an obvious reference to his suitability for the vacancy, and Simon reveals that he's aware of this but still makes no mention of Don's applying for the job. By now even Don should see that Simon is trying to tell him something, though not, of course, in so many words.

Incidentally, if Don were British, there's a good chance this conversation would never have taken place. He would assume Simon knew of his accounting background and, therefore, of his potential suitability for the vacancy. And Don would assume further that if Simon had intended to consider him for the job, he would have approached him and asked if he were interested. Because Simon had not approached him, it must have been because, for one reason or another, he was not in the running. In this way, there would have been no need for the unpleasant (for Simon) scene captured in the dialogue wherein he was forced into the embarrassing position of "telling" Don he was not a candidate. That Don did not in fact "receive" this news was beside the point as far as Simon was concerned; indeed, Simon had to be wondering why Don put him, and Don himself, in such an uncomfortable position.

For British readers, another lesson here is that since their indirectness is often entirely missed by Americans, what the British regard as true directness may only barely register with Americans. And when they're being in-your-face blunt by British standards, only then are they getting an American's attention. The lesson for Americans, meanwhile, is just the reverse: the subtle American who is pulling his punches may already be coming across quite strong

to a British man; an American who is being direct is coming across very strong; and a blunt American has just caused
a scene.

13. Sweet Time

By and large the British are not a driven people; they don't
dive into things. Indeed, to be too earnest or eager, to re-
act too quickly, generally frowned upon. Such behavior
violates that studied detachment, that bemusement or
world-weariness that is the British national attitude. It
suggests you take life too seriously, that you care a bit too
much, that you are one of those people who is liable to get
worked up about things—and people like that can't be
trusted. They're too impulsive; they lose their perspective
and their sense of balance. Nothing is *that* urgent. The
British greatly admire people who are "unflappable," that
is, completely unruffled in the midst of pandemonium.

Americans, on the other hand, are famous for their eagerness; to be driven is practically a badge of honor. Americans enjoy getting worked up about things and don't mind
showing it. It can be overdone, even in America, but there
is a much higher tolerance for conspicuous displays of energy and enthusiasm. Behavior that would qualify as driven
in England would come across as low-key in America.
Among other things, this cultural difference explains why
Americans are considered aggressive in England, and why
the British come across to Americans as having no drive.

In the dialogue, Ted gets several hints that he's coming on too strong, but he misses them all and continues to
spin in ever tighter circles. For his part, Ted is probably
wondering just what it takes to get Nicholas' attention.
Things start to go wrong at the very beginning, when a

breathless Ted catches Nicholas leaving his office. If Ted
were British, he would know better than to accost Nicholas at quitting time, know that whatever news he has, it
can certainly wait until tomorrow. But Ted isn't British
and doesn't know better, so Nicholas makes it clear that
he's going home ("I was just about to lock up"); in other
words, whatever Ted has to tell him (notice how Nicholas
never even asks), he's obviously not going to do anything
about it tonight.

When Ted persists ("I just got off the phone with the
lab"), Nicholas not only refuses the bait by not asking what
the phone call was about, but pointedly changes the subject by asking if it is still raining outside. But Ted is relent-
less (and more than a little obtuse) and keeps steady on
his course, convinced, no doubt, that once Nicholas actually hears the news, *then* he will see the urgency. But he
has misjudged his man; Nicholas is determined to stay calm
and to have this conversation some other time ("Really?
Walk with me to the elevator").

At this point even Ted should know enough to back
off; Nicholas now understands what the new development
is, and he still has quite literally not broken his stride.
Unfortunately, Ted's enthusiasm, his instinct to *do* something, has gotten the better of him, and he may also feel
encouraged when Nicholas says "Of course." (What Nicholas means here is that of course the plant managers have
to be notified—tomorrow.) If the news can wait until the
next day for Nicholas' attention, which should be obvious
even to Ted by now (but isn't), it can certainly wait over-
night for the managers. In fact, if the plant managers are
smart, and if they're British, they've already gone home.

Where does this British detachment come from? In
part it is of a piece with the British idea that reason, not

emotion, should govern behavior. People should act after thinking, not after feeling. There's almost never any need to be impulsive or to rush into things, nothing so important that it would not be better decided after careful reflection and analysis, when everyone has calmed down. This attitude is actually little more than another manifestation of that deeply held British conviction that we live in a world of finite possibilities. There are limits, you see, on what can happen in life—on what you can do, what you can be, what you can have. The way things are is pretty much the way they've always been and the way they're always going to be. No matter what we do—how long and hard we work, how much effort we make, whether or not we hear the latest development before we reach the elevator—things only change within a limited range of possibilities. We should certainly be alert to those possibilities and be prepared to exploit them to the fullest, but we should not fool ourselves; we are tinkering at the margins here, not at the core. Needless to say, this worldview takes the urgency out of most undertakings. If what you do is never going to make *that* much difference, then does it really matter whether you do it tonight or tomorrow morning?

This notion of limits is itself probably in large measure a consequence of feudalism, of a rigid hierarchy of opportunity where one lived out one's life within carefully prescribed bounds that were the glue that kept the system intact and the planet on its course. One was born into one's place in this hierarchy, and there was no more idea of changing one's place, of tinkering with or pushing the limits, than there was of changing one's gender or getting new parents. George Foster has called this belief system the "image of the limited good," and while his observations describe the traditional peasant mentality, this attitude in fact infused all levels of the feudal hierarchy up and down the social ladder. "By 'Image of the Limited Good,'" Foster writes,

> I mean that broad areas of peasant behavior are patterned in such fashion as to suggest that peas-ants view their social, economic and natural uni-verse—their total environment—as one in which all of the desired things in life, such as land, wealth, health, friendship, love, manliness and honor, re-spect and status, power and influence, security and safety—exist in finite quantity and are always in short supply, as far as the peasant is concerned. Not only do these and other "good things" exist in fi-nite and limited quantities, but in addition there is no way directly within peasant power to increase the available quantities. "Good," like land, is seen as inherent in nature—there to be divided and re-divided if necessary, but not to be augmented. (1965, 296)

It would be difficult to find sentiments further from the American view of the world. It's not necessary here to sketch yet again the American concept of unlimited op-portunity, but it is worth noting that just as British de-tachment and fatalism may derive in some measure from the legacy of feudalism, American activism and optimism can likewise be traced in part to the complete absence of a feudal tradition in that country. In any case, if you believe in infinite possibilities, life takes on greater urgency. If *anything* can happen, then there's never any excuse to ac-cept things the way they are, and always the chance—a good chance, in fact—that timely action can make a dif-ference. Under the circumstances, not to act always carries with it the possibility of some kind of loss. Waiting until tomorrow to notify the managers might be too late.

Americans also view time quite differently from Europeans, in part, perhaps, because of their sense of urgency, but also because their history is short and exceedingly compressed by European standards; indeed, by those standards, America doesn't even have any history yet. Whatever the reasons, Americans tend not to take the long view. "Most Americans," Luigi Barzini has written,

> believe (or seem to believe) that all achievements must be completely accomplished (and possibly enjoyed) within a person's lifetime…. A man must perform what he has set out to do before he dies or consider his existence wasted. This is not so in Europe, at least it wasn't so until a few years ago. Each man in the Old World knew that he was merely a link in a chain between ancestors and descendants. Life for him was a relay race. Each man received the rod from his father or his teachers and passed it on to his sons or followers. Therefore, the amount of time allowed to achieve anything—political reforms, scientific breakthroughs, personal success, fame, or the family's fortunes— was longer and more leisurely in the Old World. If a man didn't make it, his sons or grandsons might. (1983, 240–41)

Another familiar theme in American culture may be making its appearance here as well, and that is the notion of America's special destiny. From the beginning, there was a feeling that this country represented something altogether new and unprecedented in human history; it was, significantly, not just a new land or a new country—there had been many of those over the centuries—but a new world. Americans thought of and often described their country as an experiment, a chance to start over and solve once and for all the age-old political, economic, and social problems that had bedeviled the human condition from the beginning. The Old World had had more than two millennia to get things right, with very little to show for it. Now history's hopes were pinned on America, imbuing its citizens with an almost palpable sense of destiny and the corresponding compulsion to always act as quickly as possible.

Not surprisingly, Americans have always felt a sense of mission, a kind of national and individual calling to leave the world a better place. And people on a mission, like Ted in the dialogue, are usually in a hurry.

14. Business Major

The British (and much of Europe) can't seem to come to terms with the concept that business is something a person would actually have to study the way one has to study biology, for example, or statistics. Whatever you call it—commerce, trade, sales—in the British mind there isn't anything substantial or sophisticated enough under this rubric to merit serious analysis. It's not a real field or profession, after all, with a systematic body of knowledge; it's just a line of work you need a few months to get the hang of. Business is something you might very well go into after you complete your education, but it certainly wouldn't be the *subject* of your education.

While this attitude has begun to change in the era of globalization, it still lurks beneath the surface in British business circles, especially in the upper class. "Business people in the United Kingdom do not have it easy," Colin Randlesome has written.

> As a nation, the British are taught in school to deplore the vulgarity of wealth; in much of British literature, the villain of the piece is exposed as a ruthless businessman either deceiving aristocrats or exploiting workers. Prince Charles apart, the leading members of the Royal Family do not appear to be particularly interested in business, while the established Church of England gives the impression that it is actually anti-business.... In March 1992 the Bishop of London, Dr. David Hope, ascended the steps of the Royal Exchange to deliver a homily against greed, ruthlessness, and avarice. In short, the country at large has never really learned to love business. (1995, 203)

Americans are quite serious about business and essentially invented the field of business administration (the famous MBA) and the related fields of management and organizational development. They regard business as a science and have applied many of the principles of the scientific method to the study of various aspects of business. They believe business is not just a set of skills that can be acquired through practice but also constitutes a legitimate body of knowledge that has to be studied and mastered.

It is for this reason that Anna, the American in the dialogue, is no doubt taken aback when her British friend Penelope asks what her son is studying, since Anna has just said her son intends to go into business. What else would he be studying? But Penelope, who doesn't grasp that business could be a course of study, naturally assumes Anna's son must therefore be getting his degree in something else, something that has to be taught, like economics or statistics. When Anna says her son is studying business, Penelope assumes Anna has misunderstood, and she rephrases her question to make herself clearer ("But what courses is he taking?"). But to no avail.

In 1996 while business schools in America were busy granting more than eighty thousand MBAs, Oxford awarded its first MBAs ever—to forty-nine graduates. "Intellectual debate on whether business is a legitimate pursuit of knowledge [was] settled a long time ago everywhere else," the *New York Times* reported from Oxford that year, "but persuading a majority of academics in this rarefied intellectual atmosphere that there is nothing unwholesome about a business education...is an uphill fight." The *Times* article also reported on a controversial $34-million gift from Saudi billionaire Wafic Said to build a school of business at Oxford. Oxford dons rejected the offer (Ibrahim 1996, Sec. A4).

15. Looking Good

No one has ever accused the British of being starry-eyed. On the contrary, they are a cautious, skeptical people with their feet firmly planted on the ground. In a word, they are realists. In business they pride themselves on being extremely practical and would much rather be accused of being too deliberate than too enthusiastic. Hence, the unblinking, critical appraisal is expected and much admired in business; the only prudent response to any proposal or venture that looks almost too good to be true (to borrow Bill's phrase) is to assume that it is. There is never any reason to rush into things; even the most perfect of schemes is bound to have its drawbacks, which normally become apparent only over time. The safest course, therefore, is to take the incremental approach, expanding your exposure step by careful step. "Europe," Luigi Barzini has written,

> is pessimistic, prudent, practical and parsimonious. It has learned not to rush into anything, even if it is the obviously necessary or advantageous thing to do. It always prefers to wait and see. It enjoys delving into the complexity of things; the more complexities it can find the better. (1983, 14)

Americans, on the other hand, are by nature an optimistic people. While they don't necessarily expect life to always break their way, their experience has taught them that it often does. Americans sometimes try to be skeptical, but they're not very good at it; taking a dim or even a critical view of things feels somehow defeatist to them. Such a hopeful worldview, incidentally, can easily accommodate things that seem too good to be true. Their optimism tends to make Americans much less cautious and conservative than the British, especially in business. To an American, an opportunity isn't something you dissect and analyze, looking for the hidden trap; it's something you seize before it's too late, before your competition grabs it. Too much analysis and investigation lead to paralysis, or at least to a slow pace—which feels like paralysis to Americans. Americans also tend to be more spontaneous than the British, more inclined to act on the spur of the moment, on a hunch or a gut feeling, and not worry too much about the consequences: whatever they are, we can handle them.

Which brings us to Bill and Niles and the potential acquisition. Naturally, Bill has faith that it will all work out, but Niles isn't so sure, as he tries to tell Bill several times. When Niles says the acquisition "looks good from a distance," this is not in fact the endorsement Bill takes it to be, for the operative phrase here for Niles is not "Looks good" but rather "from a distance." In other words, until the acquisition is studied close-up and in great detail, it's premature to get excited about it.

Bill misreads Niles' tone and goes on to enumerate the deal's considerable advantages, starting off with an unfortunate turn of phrase ("It's almost too good to be true"), which just happens to describe Niles' sentiments exactly. In his reply ("Makes you wonder where the catch is, doesn't it?"), Niles again makes it clear the acquisition may have potential pitfalls, and he and his team will turn the deal inside out looking for the drawbacks. Bill's question ("Have you signed the letter of intent yet?") must seem very odd to Niles, for he's said twice now that he intends to proceed slowly and cautiously on this matter.

The conversation ends in one final round of misinterpretation. Assuming Niles hasn't signed because of a pitfall he's uncovered, Bill puts a final question to Niles: "Is there a problem?" Meaning only that he hasn't found one *yet*, Niles answers in the negative, whereupon Bill is relieved and assumes the deal will be consummated. What Niles means, of course, being the cautious British man, is that whether or not he has actually found a problem is of little consequence; he will find one, several perhaps, and the acquisition will have to be carefully evaluated in light of all the facts.

What accounts for American enthusiasm (as Europeans see it), for their childlike naiveté? It may stem in part from their view of the inherent or innate nature of humanity. Americans believe that people are naturally good. Sometimes they "turn out" bad, but they don't *start* that way. Accordingly, people should be trusted until they prove otherwise and should always be given the benefit of the doubt. In the American legal system, the accused is presumed innocent until proven guilty. This is why, incidentally, whenever someone does something especially bad, something evil—a word almost never used by Americans because the concept itself is so unthinkable—Americans immediately and somewhat desperately start looking for the explanation. There has to be an explanation, you see, for such behavior clearly defies logic—the logic, that is, that holds that people are naturally good. For the naturally good to suddenly turn perverse, something must have gone terribly wrong somewhere, possibly when the evildoer was a child. "You don't expect to come [across] pure evil," the American journalist Roy Gutman has observed. "I've never used the term in my writing. It's hard to bring yourself to utter the word *evil*" (in Hendrickson 1998, Sec. F7). If a journalist is uncomfortable with the concept of evil, what does that say about the average American?

As noted earlier, their largely positive (albeit limited) national experience is another reason Americans are inclined to be a naturally optimistic and trusting people. Theirs was a land of so many resources and so much opportunity that Americans didn't have to compete with others to get ahead; there was no "winners and losers" mentality, the sense that you could only succeed if someone else failed. Everyone could be a winner. Because their history was so different, Europeans often do not understand this American instinct to look on the bright side. "When things are not as they should be," Luigi Barzini writes,

> when injustice prevails, when failure crowns your efforts, when, in spite of all hopes, man shows him-

self as he always has been, Americans
are…surprised and maddened—more so than any
other people because they are so defenseless and so
ignorant of the lessons of the past. (in Pells 1997,
172)

The lessons of the European past, perhaps, but not necessarily of American history.

The British have a rather different view of humankind
and inhabit a very different moral universe. They see people
as neither naturally good nor naturally bad but equally
capable of both. In their long history they have seen the
best and worst the human race has to offer and harbor few
illusions about the darker side of human nature and are
not afraid to face it. They know that deception is not only
possible but inevitable. The only prudent course, therefore, is not to trust people until they prove trustworthy
and never to assume that others have your best interests at
heart. To give other people the benefit of the doubt is to
put yourself at a definite disadvantage, to expose yourself
to potential exploitation or manipulation. It is far wiser to
assume that people are out to take advantage of you and to
be ever alert for signs of deviousness or deception.

16. Low Key

The British appreciate understatement. They realize that
what has been said is often only half the story, that it ex-
presses only half the emotion or opinion actually held by
the speaker. They know they are expected to fill in the
rest, to add on the other, unspoken half in order to arrive
at what the speaker really meant. Moreover, they know
that when they're on the criticizing end, like Rebeccca

and Roger in the dialogue, they must be sure to leave room for this automatic add-on. Say the half, in other words, and your audience will understand the whole. But if you say the *whole*, as Roger seems inclined to do, the British will still add the "missing" half, creating a much stronger message or impression than you intended.

For Rebecca, then, saying the proposal has one or two problems means it's "full of problems" (Roger's phrase), which the folks over at the Denton Group, being British, will certainly understand. They can do the "British math," that is, one or two problems equals a boatload of trouble. There is more confusion along these lines at the end of the dialogue when Roger insists they have got to tell the Denton Group the whole story. When Rebeccca says "Of course," she doesn't mean, as Roger thinks, that she agrees that all of the problems must be spelled out; she means it has already *been* done.

Understatement is all of a piece with good manners—before anything else, the British want never to cause offense—as well as self-restraint. Keeping emotion out of polite discourse is expected and very much appreciated; indeed, it is precisely what makes such discourse polite in the first place—which is where understatement comes into play. There is much less chance you will cause a scene if you are careful to always say less than you really mean and express half the emotion you actually feel.

Understatement can also save a speaker or his or her listeners embarrassment in another way, by giving the speaker an escape should one be needed. If you say exactly what you mean or how you feel and it turns out those sentiments are not shared or otherwise appropriate, you have no avenue of retreat, and the stage is thus set for a scene—or at least embarrassment. But if you have merely implied what you mean or vaguely intimated how you feel, you can always clarify your position later if need be. Thus, it is often better to be misread than to be perfectly understood, particularly in those instances where perfect understanding might lead to unpleasantness. As G. K. Chesterton observed about his countrymen, "[The British] always say a thing in such a way that it could mean something different" (in Yapp 1988, 269).

By and large, understatement is not the American way. Americans neither use it in their own speech nor understand it when someone uses it on them. They are a nation of plain speakers, after all, where you're supposed to say what you mean—nothing less and nothing more. The safest course, therefore, when you're speaking with an American, is to always spell things out. For the most part, it's simply not possible to be *too* literal with Americans; the danger, rather, is in not being literal enough. If you say only half of what you really mean, that's exactly how much many Americans will understand. They won't fill in the missing pieces, in other words, because when *they* speak, nothing *is* missing; hence, Roger's concern that Rebecca's "one or two problems" will mislead the Denton Group, because it probably would mislead Americans.

In their own discourse, Americans prefer to err on the side of being perfectly clear, whatever the consequences. They are not afraid of confrontation, of those dreaded scenes the British will go to any lengths to avoid. They believe confrontation should be avoided if at all possible— they don't seek it out or try to provoke it (in spite of what some British believe)—but when it isn't possible, it's not the end of civilization as we know it. Confrontations can even have positive consequences; they often clear the air, for example, and they leave no doubt where everybody stands on the matter at hand. They're efficient, in other words, albeit in a brutal kind of way. The British believe it's important to know where everyone stands, too, of course; they just don't think it should require a confrontation to find this out. There are other, more civilized ways to get people to state their opinions. For the British, a confrontation represents a breakdown in communication; for Americans, it's merely communication with the volume turned up.

17. Taking Advantage

This is going to be very hard to explain to Carl, but Camilla actually disagrees with him on every point; that is, she does not intend to postpone the talks or manipulate events to be able to dictate the terms of the merger. When she asks him if the reason for postponing the meeting is to gain an advantage, she's just checking to make sure he doesn't have some other motive in mind, a motive she might find acceptable. When he confirms he doesn't ("Right"), she then makes one further inquiry to make sure she understands his dubious logic, asking whether his goal is to be able to dictate the terms of the merger. When he answers "Exactly," then she knows she will have to oppose him, though he, of course, will be astonished to find this out. In his defense, there aren't many clues in the dialogue, except for her early remark about the drop in earnings making things "a bit sticky" for BMG. To Carl, Camilla is merely describing a positive development in the merger talks, but Camilla is actually suggesting the opposite, implying that now (when things are "sticky") may not be the proper time to negotiate with the other party.

Why is Camilla reluctant to proceed? Because it would

be unsporting, unfair, or, to get right down to it, ungentle-
manly to take advantage of BMG when it is weak and vulnerable. Kicking the competition when it's down simply is
not done. Or, if it is done, it is not soon forgotten. Rushing in to take advantage of BMGs' misfortune might give
Camilla's company a leg up for the short term, but the
memory of their unscrupulous behavior would taint the
company for years. And that could prove very costly. Carl
has come smack up against the British notion of fair play,
which is deeply embedded in their culture. The British are
the people who invented the maxim "What matters is not
whether you win or lose, but how you play the game." This
doesn't mean the British don't like to win—they can, in
fact, be fiercely competitive—but it's important to win in
a fair fight. Winning when the other side is at a disadvantage is a hollow victory.

The notion of fair play is of a piece with the tradition
of business as a kind of gentleman's game or hobby, the
club we all belong to, and is an essential part of the code
of the gentleman. People who are brought up well don't
take advantage of each other; it's bad manners and bad
form. We all need to make a profit, and we all can so long
as we agree to abide by certain rules and certain limits.
The fortunes of the players may wax and wane within these
limits, but as long as we all play fair, then we will all prosper.

Americans have never regarded business as a game,
and especially not as a game where everyone has to win.
On the contrary, business is more like war, with winners
and losers, and it uses similar tactics. If the enemy is weak,
seize the moment, for he would certainly do the same if
the tables were turned. Winning may not be everything to
Americans, but it's very high on the list of desirable things.

This doesn't mean they countenance winning by any means, but it is certainly acceptable to exploit a rival's weaknesses. In America business is not for the faint of heart; it is necessary to be cutthroat on occasion, and one of the requirements of a successful businessperson is an instinct for the jugular. One should still try to be fair, of course, but that doesn't mean one can't be ruthless. Needless to say, American business practices often strike the British as crude, even brutal, while the British, from the American perspective, don't really have the stomach for business.

It's possible, incidentally, that even a British company would seize the opportunity described in this dialogue, but one imagines a certain amount of hesitation and soul-searching as everyone agonizes over whether or not it's the right thing to do. For Americans, one suspects, the soul-searching would not be prolonged and the agony would likewise be minimal.

2

Americans and the French

Dialogues 18–34

Americans have no capacity for abstract thought and make bad coffee.

> —Georges Clemenceau
> French Prime Minister

In his pithy way, Clemenceau got a great deal right about the differences between Americans and the French. The former are enthusiastically unintellectual (though not as *anti*-intellectual as the French sometimes think) and somewhat puritanical (taking a dim view of sensual indulgence, for example), while the French, of course, lionize great thinkers and practically invented joie de vivre. If Clemenceau had permitted an American rejoinder, it would no doubt have gone something like this: "The French think too much and are obsessed with food."

Of the three cultural pairings in this book, Americans and the French surely have the least in common. While Americans normally see something of themselves in the behavior of the Germans and occasionally in the British, they see little they recognize in the French. Americans understand the British and the Germans to some extent and vice versa, but the same cannot be said for Americans and the French. Indeed, Americans don't seem to understand the French at all, though whether the French understand the Americans is harder to say. They may—the French are quite clever—but what is more likely is that they haven't given Americans enough thought to have figured them out. They *could* understand Americans, if they wanted to, but they don't seem to have cared to. Americans shouldn't take this personally, by the way, for the French don't appear to have thought that much about *any* culture other than their own.

Does this mean the French really are the snobs and egoists they have been rumored to be down through the ages? Perhaps—most cultural stereotypes, both the critical and the complimentary, have a germ of truth—but it is probably fairer to say that the French are extremely proud of their culture and their heritage. If this pride occasionally lapses into chauvinism (the word comes from the name of the fanatically loyal French soldier, Nicolas Chauvin), then so be it.

Why should the Franco-American cultural gap be so much wider than that between the other cultures in this book? One obvious reason would be that while many immigrants to America were from England and Germany, far fewer came from France. France, moreover, has a distinctly

Mediterranean or southern European, a distinctly *Latin*, cast to its culture, which makes it not only different from the United States but from most of northern Europe as well, including England and Germany. The British and the Germans have as hard a time with France (and vice versa) as do Americans. It may also be that of the three European cultures in these pages, France had the oldest and most deeply entrenched feudal tradition. As noted earlier, much of what made America American was the rejection of certain characteristics that made Europe European, and foremost among the latter was the inherent inequality of the class system, which was nowhere stronger than in France. "Considering we are a republic," Ludwig Bemelmans once wrote of the French, "we have more regard for privilege than any nation on earth" (in Yapp 1988, 143).

Americans love France, incidentally. They realize the French condescend to and patronize them, normally two of the worst things you can do to an American, but they somehow accept this behavior from the French, probably because Americans are not singled out. Americans find the French terribly sophisticated and worldly and are openly in awe of many aspects of their culture. Americans know they are almost boorish by comparison and cheerfully accept their inferior status. They forgive all manner of offensive traits in the French because of their terrific sense of style. "When they die," one nineteenth-century wit observed, "good Americans go to Paris" (James 1986, 8). (This sentiment was later embellished by Oscar Wilde, who added that when *bad* Americans died, they went to America.) Admire them though they may, Americans aren't fooled by the French and do not forgive them their unprincipled opportunism in foreign affairs, such as their cozying up to Saddam Hussein or Muammar Qaddafi. (France wouldn't allow American jets to fly over French airspace on their mission to bomb Libya). To many Americans, the French certainly have very good taste, but one must never trust them.

The French, meanwhile, are greatly amused by the Americans—when they aren't totally exasperated by them. They resent U.S. power and influence, of course—it takes the spotlight off where it rightly belongs—but they find Americans endlessly engaging and admire their spirit. The French wouldn't stoop to be jealous of Americans (or anyone else), but they do envy them all the attention they get.

Dialogues

18. Knowing Your Stuff

BILL: I hear Mme. Masson's going to represent us at the meeting.

JACQUES: It's a good choice.

BILL: Is she a good speaker?

JACQUES: I suppose so. She's quite knowledgeable and very well-read.

BILL: How do you mean?

JACQUES: She's well versed in philosophy, literature, history.

BILL: But does she know her stuff?

JACQUES: Her stuff?

BILL: You know—the business?

19. Bothering the Chief

TOM: I think we'll need to hire two part-time people to help us plan the conference.

CLAUDINE: Yes. We're running out of time, and this conference has to go well.

TOM: I could speak to human resources today.

CLAUDINE: Did you already mention this to M. Marceau?

TOM: The chief? I didn't want to bother him with this. He's busy getting ready for that sales meeting. Besides, it's your division. He'll agree to anything you say.

CLAUDINE: Yes. I'm sure he'll approve.

TOM: Good. Then I'll call human resources this afternoon.

20. Working Late

PAT: We could finish this if we stayed late tonight.

YVES: Has the deadline changed?

PAT: I don't think so, but we're so close.

YVES: Yes, it will be nice to start a new project.

PAT: How late can you stay?

YVES: Me? I'm leaving at quitting time.

21. Time to Redesign

PAM: How much longer do you think it will take?

ANDRE: Probably two months, especially if we add the timing feature. And another month to do the redesign of the case.

PAM: You're redesigning the case?

ANDRE: It will look much sleeker.

PAM: You know Systems Inc. is launching Technomax early next month.

ANDRE: Of course, but it's just not as good a product.

PAM: Maybe not, but it does at least 75 percent of what ours will do.

ANDRE: Precisely.

22. Withholding

DEBBIE: Giscard's desperate. He can't find a new supplier for the titanium bearings.

FRANCINE: I know. He never should have relied so much on Levesque Inc. I warned him.

DEBBIE: This means we'll probably be idle over here for at least a day. Somebody's got to know another supplier.

FRANCINE: Oh, I do, actually. He's the same guy who supplies us with adhesives. Working for Giscard would drive him crazy.

DEBBIE: Never mind. You've got to tell Giscard.

23. Religion and Politics

SUZANNE: Hey, Pierre. Come and join us.

PIERRE: How are you, Suzanne? Bonjour, François.

SUZANNE: François and I were just discussing religion. I told him it was dangerous, but he never listens.

PIERRE: Dangerous?

SUZANNE: You know. Some people take it quite seriously.

PIERRE: Of course.

SUZANNE: No use risking a friendship over it though, is there?

PIERRE: How do you mean?

SUZANNE: You know, disagreeing.

24. Le Clos Is Late

PHILIPPE: Le Clos' data is late again.

MARCIA: Let's give him another day. Something must have happened.

PHILIPPE: Something *always* happens. It's
been six months now. There's
definitely a pattern here.

MARCIA: He tries hard, though. I'm sure
he's doing his best.

PHILIPPE: Why do you say that?

MARCIA: He told me how much this
contract means to him.

25. Call Me Later

JEAN PAUL: Carl, I haven't seen you in such a
long time. Sit down.

CARL: Thanks anyway. I didn't realize
you weren't free. Sorry I didn't
call but I didn't expect to be out
this way.

JEAN PAUL: Never mind. We need to catch up
on your news. Do you know La
Roche, here? He was just filling
me in on the BDM negotiations.
You'd find it interesting, actually.

CARL: How do you do. I don't want to
interrupt, but call me later, Jean
Paul, when you have a chance.

26. At the Window

CAROL: I have some great news for supervisors.

MICHELLE: What is it?

CAROL: I've found some new software that puts customer account information right at the teller's station, at the teller's fingertips.

MICHELLE: Do you mean tellers will be able to access customer accounts directly, without calling in a supervisor?

CAROL: Exactly. It's really efficient. I'm sure customers will be very impressed with how fast they get answers.

MICHELLE: No doubt.

27. Lunch with Gallimard

MARCEL: It's all arranged. Gallimard will meet us for lunch tomorrow at noon.

JOYCE: Finally we get to meet him. What's the plan?

MARCEL: He likes Chez Manuel, in Montmartre.

JOYCE: That should work. I have another appointment at two, but if we finish lunch by 1:30 I'll make it.

MARCEL: Maybe I should try to reschedule lunch for another day.

JOYCE: Are you kidding? After all the trouble it's taken to set this up?

28. The Thinker

TODD: Did Henri turn in his draft yet?

GERARD: No, he's still working on it. You know Henri, always thinking and pondering.

TODD: But I needed that draft last week.

GERARD: He never meets his deadlines. But his ideas are really wonderful. We had a great talk yesterday. He was saying that...

TODD: I've complained twice about him to M. Cardin, but he doesn't do anything.

GERARD: You've complained? Why?

29. Mistakes

DARRYL: Andre said there are some mistakes in the specs.

JEAN CLAUDE: Andre? How did he get involved?

DARRYL: I have no idea. Where is that spec sheet, anyway?

JEAN CLAUDE: You want to look at it?

DARRYL: Just to make sure.

JEAN CLAUDE: Andre must be upset about something.

DARRYL: Yeah. The specs!

30. Running Late

CLAUDE: M. LeBlanc will see you in ten
minutes.

JANET: I hope everything's okay. We had
an appointment at nine, twenty
minutes ago.

CLAUDE: Actually, he's still meeting with
his marketing director. I can show
you in, if you like.

JANET: Oh no. I don't want to interrupt
them. Must be really important,
eh?

CLAUDE: How do you mean?

31. Sales Figures

PETER: We should get our second set of
sales figures tomorrow.

BRIGITTE: Yes.

PETER: Then we'll know how we're
doing.

BRIGITTE: After two quarters?

PETER: And whether we'll need to make
any changes.

BRIGITTE: Changes?

PETER: You know, in case we're losing
market share.

32. Madame X

ANN: I love these old-style elevators.

ALAIN: Yes. These old buildings have a lot of charm. Bonjour, madame.

MADAME: Bonjour, monsieur.

ANN: Who was that woman? I see her every time I visit you here.

ALAIN: Yes, she lives on the fifth floor. I ride with her almost every day.

ANN: What's her name?

ALAIN: Her name? No idea.

33. Dinner on Friday

M. JAVERT: I was wondering if you and Mrs. Johnson could have dinner with us on Friday. My wife is eager to meet my new colleague.

MR. JOHNSON: That would be very nice.

M. JAVERT: I'll get back to you with the details.

MR. JOHNSON: Let us know if we can bring anything.

M. JAVERT: How do you mean?

34. Meeting Jeanette

MONIQUE: Here comes a friend of mine, Jeanette. I haven't seen her in a long time.

PATRICIA: Oh.

MONIQUE: This won't take too long.

PATRICIA: Take your time. I enjoy meeting your friends.

MONIQUE: Excuse me?

pearance of those sensibilities in the first place. For the most part, young countries like the United States are too busy wrestling with more immediate, practical problems—establishing laws and governments, building roads and bridges, developing agriculture, trade, and industry—to have either the time or the inclination for poetry and symphonies. Until a society has its physical infrastructure and economic house in order, the adornment of the mind is a luxury few can afford. "So great is the call for talents of all sorts in the active use of professional and other business in America," a prominent judge wrote in 1819, "that few of our ablest men have leisure to devote exclusively to literature or the fine arts…. This obvious reason will explain why we have so few professional authors, and those not among our ablest men" (Boorstin 1958, 314–15).

19. Bothering the Chief

If an American and a French person are going to do business together or work in the same organization, they will need to know about the concept of power distance. More to the point, they will need to know that their respective views on power in the workplace are in fact poles apart. Power distance, as identified and defined by the Dutch sociologist Geert Hofstede, refers to the attitude of a society toward the inherent inequalities in life, and in particular toward the fact that certain people have significantly more or less power and influence than other people. In one of its most conspicuous forms (and the one on display in this dialogue), power distance affects what people consider to be the proper roles and behavior of managers and subordinates in the workplace and in the business world.

The American, Tom, for reasons discussed below, has a somewhat looser way with power, assuming that the name of the game here is not to bow and scrape to one's superiors but to get things done (which is in the end what really matters to and will please those same superiors). Moreover, he also assumes that people who have had power officially delegated to them are free to exercise it without further consultation. Both assumptions, it turns out, are invalid in the French workplace, though Tom misses the cues that tell him this. The first comes when Claudine asks if he has checked with M. Marceau, their boss, for his blessing to hire the new people. To Tom this is an idle, even odd question, since this is Claudine's division and her boss will "agree to anything" she says. Moreover, since it is her division and since her boss expects her to manage it—and especially since he's "busy getting ready for the sales meeting"—he won't appreciate being "bothered" about such a small matter.

Small to Tom, perhaps (and to other Americans), but probably not to Claudine or M. Marceau. On the whole, power is much more closely held and jealously guarded in France, and people such as Claudine who have the authority on paper to make decisions normally check with their superiors before acting, even on the most routine matters, as a kind of courtesy and ritual deference. Tom's assumption that Claudine can make this decision on her own is in fact inaccurate and now leads him to make a second mistake. When Claudine says she's "sure [the boss] will approve" hiring the part-time help, Tom takes this to mean that the decision has been made and he can contact human resources. But what Claudine really means is that she's sure the boss will approve *when she asks him,* and that to take any action on this matter before then would be inappropriate. M. Marceau, in short, will not find it bothersome to be asked about this matter; he will regard it, rather, as the courtesy due someone in his position.

Not surprisingly, France is what is known as a high power-distance culture. In Geert Hofstede's survey of power distance in 39 countries, France was ranked the highest of all European countries in this area (and number 8 overall). The United States, by contrast, was ranked 26th (Germany, 30th and Great Britain, 31st). High power-distance cultures accept that inequalities in power, influence, and status are natural or existential. Everyone accepts that certain people will have more power and influence than others in much the same way they accept that some people are more intelligent or better looking than others. Those with power tend to emphasize it, hold it close, not delegate or share it, and try to distinguish themselves as much as possible from those who do not have power. They are, however, expected to accept the responsibilities that go with power, especially that of looking after those beneath them. Subordinates are not expected to take initiative and are closely supervised. "Top [French] executives are strongly autocratic in their style of management," Robert Moran notes. "These executives practice strict, top-down management, voicing their wishes to subordinates who then further transmit them down the line" (1992, 32). It was a Frenchman, don't forget, the great Sun King Louis XIV, who delivered himself of what is probably the most famous statement ever made about power: "L'état, c'est moi" ("I am the State").

This does not mean, incidentally, that French subordinates take all this lying down, meekly serving their masters and grateful for their sufferance. There is, in fact, a kind of guerrilla war in France between superiors and sub-

ordinates, so that while bosses may wield their considerable power freely and shamelessly, their proud subordinates
often bristle at being told what to do and are constantly
on the lookout for ways to thwart management. As David
Hickson and Derek Pugh have noted,

> Culturally, the French approach [to managing and
> organizing] is distinctive, indeed unique, in the
> tension it embodies between looking for and re-
> sponding to a strong, authoritative lead, while in-
> dividualistically resisting the encroachment of au-
> thority. No other Latin nation has this tension to
> this degree. (1995, 75)

High power distance is, of course, all of a piece with an
aristocratic society, where power is centralized in the hands
of a few. It is also emblematic of the family dynamic where
a strong father has the last word (and a good many before
that). Richard Pells has pointed out that "most European
businesses [were] family run.... The old guard preferred a
benevolent paternalism to unbridled competition. For its
beneficiaries, this system may have seemed idyllic, but in
fact it was inflexible [and] encouraged authoritarian decision making..." (1997, 192).

Americans tend to be low power-distance types. They
see inequalities in power and influence as man-made and
largely artificial; it is not natural, though it may be convenient and even necessary, that some people have power
over others. Those with power, therefore, mindful of the
inherent unfairness of the situation, tend to de-emphasize
it; they try to minimize the differences between themselves
and subordinates and even to redistribute power as much
as possible, through delegating responsibility and reward-
ing initiative. In such cultures, the best organizational

charts are the flattest ones, and the best bosses are invisible, flexing their managerial muscle (i.e., drawing attention to their power) only as a last resort. Subordinates neither like nor expect close supervision, which has come to
be known as micromanagement—and which, by the way,
is expected and normally appreciated in most high power-
distance cultures.

The Americans' attitude toward power derives in large
part from their acute discomfort with inequality in any
form, whether of power or wealth or, most importantly,
opportunity. It was in large part to escape inequality that
the republic came into being in the first place, so it is not
surprising that the egalitarian ethos, the notion that no
one is inherently superior to anyone else, should have been
enshrined at the core of the American national character.
Most cultures value equality, of course, including France—
Liberté, Égalité, Fraternité were the rallying cries of the
French Revolution—but none have made it the cornerstone of their society in quite the way Americans have.
Nothing raises an American's ire more quickly than people
who act as if they're better than other people, who "lord it
over" others, as Americans sometimes put it. There were
to be no lords of any kind in America, starting most con-
spicuously at the top with the president, who was quite
pointedly not a king. "Americans dislike being made to
feel inferior," Edward T. Hall and Mildred Reed Hall have
written,

> and bristle at any system of arbitrary social ranking
> independent of achievement. They are uncomfort-
> able with class systems such as those in France or
> England. The American belief in equality makes
> Americans dislike those who act superior or con-

descending. Even influential people usually make an effort to appear approachable. For example, the manager who puts his feet on the desk, works in his shirt-sleeves, and invites everyone to call him by his first name is trying to show that he too is a member of the team. (1990, 150)

20. Working Late

This dialogue is about the place that work should occupy in the scheme of things, and in particular the balance between the competing demands of making a living and enjoying life. In France it's no contest; enjoying life wins hands down. Joie de vivre, as the French say, is not so much an ideal as it is an obligation. Witness the six-week vacations, the inordinate attention lavished on the preparation and presentation of food, the obsession with sensuality, the profound importance of style. Enjoying life is a serious responsibility—there's even a government minister in charge of quality of life—and those poor souls who somehow manage not to, almost never fail for lack of trying. "I do envy these Europeans the comfort they take," Mark Twain wrote on his first trip abroad.

> When the work of the day is done, they forget it. Some of them go, with wife and children, to a beer hall and sit quietly and genteely drinking a mug or two of ale and listening to music; others walk the streets, others drive the avenues; others assemble in the great ornamental squares in the early evening to enjoy the sight and fragrance of flowers.... They go to bed moderately early and sleep well. (1895, 187)

Needless to say, in a culture where living well is an art, work is merely the means to an end, drudgery, a necessary evil about which the less said the better. This is not to say the French are lazy or irresponsible or even that they don't take their work seriously—they are, in fact, among Europe's hardest workers—but only that they see nothing inherently good in working any longer or harder than they have to. They will rise to the occasion in a genuine emergency, but anything less does not justify staying after hours or coming in on the weekend. "French people believe there is more to life than the job," John Mole has written.

> Hard work is admired but workaholism is not. While the affectation of regularly working late is creeping into Parisian working habits, there is a clear division between private and business lives. Weekends and vacation days, sport, cultural activities and family life are very important. (1995, 27)

You will find virtually no glorification of work in France, nothing about work being somehow noble or good or building character or any other such nonsense. Work is work, *travailler* in French, from which we get the English word *travail*. Still not convinced? Then consider this: *travailler* comes from the Vulgar Latin *tripaliare*, which means to torture someone with a three-pronged instrument. The French have romanticized many things, but work isn't one of them.

In the dialogue the American, Pat, makes the mistake (in France, anyway) of appearing to value work for its own sake; that is, he seems to want to stay late merely to finish the project. Naturally, this prompts Yves to ask if the deadline has changed, for in Yves' world there could be no other reason to work past quitting time. When he learns the

deadline has not changed, Yves must wonder what's gotten into Pat.

What *has* gotten into Pat? Is he a workaholic? Out to
impress the boss? Or does he simply need to get a life?
What's gotten into Pat, of course, is his culture, specifi-
cally the American work ethic which teaches, among other
things, that work is intrinsically good, that it is more than
simply the means to do what matters in life but is itself *one*
of the things that matters. Work is a practical necessity, of
course, but Americans have always felt that it was somehow important to work, that work gave meaning and purpose to life. Work may not be who you are, but it becomes
something more than merely what you do. Even if an
American's job is not the whole of his or her identity, however, it is certainly a larger part of that identity than it is
for many Europeans. It is no accident that when two Americans first meet, one of the first things they ask each other
is "What do you do?" for that is the quickest way of knowing who the other person is. Those who don't work in the
United States—referred to, tellingly, as the idle rich—get
very little respect, so little, in fact, that they usually end
up working anyway so that their lives, as the expression
has it, will have "amounted to something." At-home moth-
ers suffer from the same syndrome. In one survey, 75 percent of Americans said they would continue working even
if they were given the money to live comfortably for the
rest of their lives.

In such a scheme, Pat's idea of staying late or coming
in on the weekend to finish a project would not be quite
the sacrifice it is in Yves' culture, where work does not
have this particular significance. Indeed, staying late to
finish a project ahead of time could even have a certain
appeal to Pat or, at the very least, offer a small measure of

satisfaction. For Pat, staying late clearly represents something entirely different than it does for Yves, which is why each speaker leaves this conversation shaking his head: Pat annoyed because the French have no drive, Yves shocked at Americans who don't know enough to leave work on time.

The American attitude toward work is in large part a consequence of the Protestant, or Puritan, ethic with "its strong accent on work and wealth accumulation," as Carl Degler has noted,

> [and which] bestowed religious sanction upon business enterprise.... To the Puritan, a Christian's work was a part of his offering to God. "As soon as ever a man begins to look toward God and the way of his Grace," the Reverend John Cotton taught, "he will not rest til he find out some warrantable calling and employment." To work hard is to please God. As Cotton Mather, the grandson of [John] Cotton, said at the end of the century, "Would a man Rise by his Business? I say, then let him Rise to his Business.... Let your Business ingross the most of your time." (1984, 7)

The Puritan ethic not only extolled work, it also denigrated play. Leisure, idleness, the pursuit of pleasure—none of these were very close to God, and to this day Americans have a deep ambivalence about enjoying themselves too much. At the very least, pleasure and relaxation must be earned (through work, of course), and even then too much of either makes Americans feel guilty. In *Working At Play*, her history of vacations in the United States, Cindy Aron has written of "the evil that was associated with leisure. For throughout the last half of the nineteenth cen-

tury leisure remained...tinged with its Puritan heritage:
Those at leisure were idle and idleness meant trouble."
Aron also describes what she calls a "persistent dilemma"
in American culture:

> How to enjoy leisure without jeopardizing the com-
> mitment to work. What is compelling about the
> history of vacations is the constancy with which
> Americans have struggled with the notion of tak-
> ing off time from work.... Americans engaged in a
> love/hate battle with their vacations—both want-
> ing to take them and fearing the consequences.
> Relaxing did not come easily to American men and
> women who continued to use their leisure in the
> performance of various sorts of work—religious
> work, intellectual work, therapeutic work. Leisure
> and labor remained complicated and troubling cat-
> egories. (in Yardley 1999, 2)

Americans also have more choice over what they do in
life than does the typical French person (though this is
now changing in France). When you are free to choose
the work you do, you are more likely to be committed to it
and to identify with it.

The French have had less choice than Americans regarding job or career. Historically, one simply did the work
associated with the class or subclass one was born into.
"European life offered very little choice to most men,"
Daniel Boorstin notes. "They had no freedom but to per-
form the tasks to which their own family station assigned
them" (1958, 199).

Under the aristocratic tradition and centuries of feudalism in France (and throughout most of Europe), the
only people who worked were those who had to, the so-

called "working class," the name used to distinguish them from the classes that typically did not work, such as the gentry and those in the trades (who were slightly more respectable because they didn't work quite as hard as the working class, and they didn't work directly for others). There were no illusions that work was somehow ennobling; on the contrary, work was what the lower orders did so the nobles wouldn't have to work. Nor was work something you did to improve your lot or get ahead. It was, rather, something you did to improve the lot of others.

Even now, the French education system steers young people into distinctive tracks at an early age, long before most people have decided what they want to do, and it is difficult to later choose a future outside of one's track. That same system, famous for its *grandes écoles,* or elite institutions of higher learning, has also created a decidedly unegalitarian workplace, effectively roping off the higher ranks of employment to only people from the right background with the right connections. All of these factors— family background, kind and level of education, social class—combine to limit the average person's choices when he or she decides upon employment. In the end, many French choose their work on the basis of what is available to them or what their family has always done rather than what they've decided they want to do with their life. As a result, the French don't identify closely with their jobs, which explains, incidentally, why the subject of one's work doesn't come up that often in French conversation. Knowing what people do doesn't reveal anything important about them, or at least not anything *they* think is important.

Finally, as noted earlier, the role of the family looms larger in the typical French person's life than it does for most Americans, which may be another explanation for

the different emphasis on work. "Family time is so important in France," Gilles Asselin and Ruth Mastron note,

> that people rarely sacrifice it for additional in-
> come.... For the French, the additional income
> does not make up for the loss of time relaxing with
> family and friends. French employees may simply
> refuse to work overtime or on weekends, and this
> cultural position is reinforced by laws limiting the
> demands employers can make. (2001, 61)

21. Time to Redesign

The French are more interested in designing than producing; they much prefer thinking to doing and are, in fact,
much better at theorizing than at execution. The mun-
dane realities of manufacturing and selling can't begin to
compete with the thrill of analysis and conceptualizing.
They are, after all, famous for asking whether what works
in practice also works in theory—and judging accordingly.
"The French are brilliant intellectually," Theodore Zeldin
has noted, "but weak in common sense" (in Hill 1995,
79). They have a related tendency to prefer what is complex to what is simple; it gives their intellect much more
of a workout, which they find extremely satisfying. Indeed,
they are not at all beyond making the simple *into* the complex, seemingly just for that reason. They are not a practical people, in short, for which they make no apologies,
and are the first to admit that they don't live in the real
world, at least no more than they have to. The prevailing
national sentiment is to let other nationalities—the
Americans, say, or the Germans—be practical, while the
French occupy the higher ground, worrying mainly about

beauty and truth. If you press them (and not all that hard), they will tell you this is their destiny. "French people enjoy abstract thought, theory, and formulas," John Mole writes, "and a degree of logic and analysis which often seems impractical to pragmatic thinkers like the British or the Dutch. Eclecticism is not an important element of mental discipline and there is a mistrust of pure pragmatism" (1995, 24).

The dialogue illustrates one of the many forms this sentiment takes: the notion that in business one should not worry so much about whether one's product is competitive, so long as it's well designed (overdesigned, critics of the French would say) and elegant. Or, to put it more charitably, if a product is well designed and elegant, it *will* be competitive. In any case, worrying too much about profit and the commercial side of things is somehow unseemly, a job for little people with small minds. "Profit is a fallout of the system," one American executive based in France has observed. "It's nice to have it, but not the main preoccupation.... The idea is that if you have a technical advance and an interesting product, [people] will want it" (Mole 1995, 231). Naturally, if a product can be both beautiful *and* turn a profit, no one will object, but if it can't, then one should opt for "sleek" (to use Andre's word from the dialogue). "France is the only country," the poet Paul Valéry once observed, "where considerations of pure form, a concern with form for its own sake, have kept a dominant position" (Gramont 1969, 301). And what about the customer, you say? What if the customer doesn't appreciate the difference? Then the customer is an idiot.

While the French are busy pursuing perfection more or less for its own sake, Americans are busy being pragmatic; they're quite happy, in fact, to leave thinking to the French and concentrate on doing. "[Americans] will habitually prefer the useful to the beautiful," Alexis de Tocqueville observed, "and they will require that the beautiful should be useful" (1984, 18). Americans are similarly no-nonsense when it comes to business. Business isn't about truth and beauty; it's about profit. And profit is a function of being competitive. In the real world you can't have it both ways; you can get your product on the market or you can continue to perfect it. In the former case, it will sell; in the latter, it will become more and more beautiful.

The dialogue begins with the American, Pam, concerned about how much longer it's going to take to design a certain new product. If she were French, Pam would know you don't hurry designers; a good design takes as long as it takes. She is not reassured when Andre tells her the case for the new product is actually being *re*designed. When Pam asks why, she gets a very logical reason from the French point of view "It will look much sleeker," which amounts almost to a non sequitur from her perspective. Tired of beating around the bush, Pam now brings up her strongest point, explaining to Andre that the delay he has described—a delay, don't forget, with no real payoff as far as Pam is concerned—means the competition will beat them to the market.

With one comment after another, Pam is appealing to instincts that Andre simply doesn't have: the profit motive, timeliness, competition. Her final ploy, explaining that Technomax's product "does at least 75 percent" of what Andre's will do, is, of course, an argument for Andre's position, not against it. After all, where perfection is the goal, as it is in French design, cutting corners has very little appeal.

A "puzzling feature of the French persona in business," Richard Hill writes,

> [is] their ability to allow their spirit of Cartesianism to smother…common sense. As an American businessman remarked to a reporter in the mid-60's: "The Frenchman, by inclination and education, mistrusts simple things and tends to over-complicate." The French taste for complicating things may of course reflect a peculiarly Gothic form of perfectionism: French design is often idiosyncratic and clever but not always practical. But the predilection also suggests simple intellectual conceit, accompanied at times by a rather charming and childlike desire to show off. (1994, 54–55)

French engineers are particularly good at this. For them the product is almost an end in itself, a perfect widget, with perfection, not profitability, as the ultimate aim. "French engineers design systems that aim at being 100 percent perfect," one observer has noted. "If you ask them to design something fast, such as a computerized billing system that is only 80 percent perfect but will have a short time-to-market, they won't be much interested" (Platt 1995, 213). It's not surprising, incidentally, that this mentality should prevail in French business, for the French respect math and science, hence engineers, above all other disciplines. Senior managers in French manufacturing companies are more likely to have an engineering background than any other.

The practical streak in American culture is in part a legacy of life in the New World, where new and unprecedented circumstances presented Americans with a constant stream of challenges and problems that demanded

immediate solutions. Under these conditions what was
needed was not something complicated or elegant or fully
thought through, but something that worked. Simple was
better mainly because it was faster, and speed was of the
essence. "The man of action," Tocqueville observed,

> is frequently obliged to content himself with the
> best he can get, because he would never accom-
> plish his purpose if he chose to carry every detail
> to perfection. He has perpetually occasion to rely
> on ideas which he has not had leisure to search to
> the bottom; for he is much more frequently aided
> by the [timeliness] of an idea than by its strict ac-
> curacy. (1984, 165)

Whether or not they had the inclination, in other
words, early Americans didn't have the time to think.

The gulf between designers and producers, between
R&D and manufacturing, exists in the United States too,
of course, but it is normally not as wide. One possible explanation is that specialization was never as advanced in
America as it was in France, where the history of expert
craftsmanship and the subsequent power of the guilds made
cooperation among craftsmen virtually impossible. American companies have their share of specialists and even
competing divisions, but there is a sense of working together for the common good that is often lacking in French
enterprises (see Dialogue 22, "Withholding," pages 103–
104 and below).

22. Withholding

"The French," Richard Hill has written, "have a visceral
need to assert their individuality." French individualism,

much different from the American variety, is a combination of what the French call *egoism*, or self-centeredness,
and *amour propre*, very high self-regard or self-esteem. It is
the quality responsible for that arrogance or air of superiority that is perhaps the most common complaint foreigners
make about the French. It is noteworthy, in the present context, that most French do not regard this characterization
as a criticism. "Most self-respecting French people are short
on modesty," Hill continues, "even disarmingly conceited
about their intellectual prowess. I say 'disarmingly' because
they are quite happy to admit it: an American publishing
friend of mine had one of his [French] employees concede,
straightfaced, that 'We French are full of ourselves, and jus-
tifiably so'" (1994, 56). The French, it should be noted, not
only make such claims for themselves personally but also
for their language and their culture. "As happy as God in
France" is a phrase children learn at an early age.

As a practical matter, their amour propre makes it very
difficult for the French to work together with others, or
even to trust them. Cooperation, compromise, give-and-
take—all of these involve setting one's ego aside or, worse,
subsuming it under someone else's ego, both of which are
anathema in France. "Professional relationships between
colleagues are founded more on rivalry than collaboration,"
John Mole notes. "This begins in the highly competitive
school environment which is based on getting over a series of ever higher hurdles. Learning to collaborate to solve
problems is not an educational goal. Far from refreshing,
people find it disconcerting when others do not compete"
(1995, 20).

In other cultures there is something called the greater
good, the idea of sacrificing your own needs or desires for a
cause bigger than yourself, but in France there is no good

greater than the individual. Ego "is an inevitable by-product of [French] individualism," Hill has written.

> Every French national is a little law unto him or
> herself. They have an autonomy born as much of
> self-absorption as of *amour propre*. This means
> among other things that "putting themselves in the
> other chap's shoes," as the English would do, does
> not come to them naturally.... (1995, 87)

It is through this lens, then, that we should examine
Francine's behavior in the dialogue. We learn in the first
line that someone named Giscard is in a tight spot. While
this news apparently constitutes a call to action to the
American, Debbie, who believes you should reach out to
colleagues in need, this is not how it would normally strike
a French person, whose first response would be that
Giscard's bind is his own doing. Giscard himself would no
doubt feel the same way, incidentally, and not be expecting a helping hand from Francine.

For her part, meanwhile, Francine has to be wondering why Debbie has raised the matter with her in the first
place, since it clearly has nothing to do with either of them.
She tries to make this point in her response when she says
"I warned him," by which she means that although she
was in no way obliged to, she actually did Giscard a favor
and told him about Levesque. If Giscard is foolish enough
to ignore advice so nobly and selflessly given, then that's
his problem, not Francine's. And certainly not Debbie's.

Much to Francine's surprise—and no doubt, to her
growing annoyance—Debbie is still determined to rescue
Giscard. Since appealing to Francine's sympathy for
Giscard has apparently not worked, Debbie now appeals
to Francine's self-interest, pointing out that their own di-

vision will be idled if Giscard's problem isn't solved. Debbie thinks she's broken through when Francine announces she has information (the name of another supplier), and the dialogue ends with Debbie's insistence (and her assumption) that Francine pass this name on to Giscard.

She won't, of course, which she has clearly indicated when she says that working with Giscard would drive her source crazy. After all, if the supplier Francine knows (and may need to call on in the future) wouldn't like working with Giscard, and if he was hooked up with Giscard thanks to Francine, that could spell trouble for her. Perhaps Francine's division will be idled by her hoarding of this information, but this situation pits the greater good of the company against what's best for Francine. And for the Francines of the world, this is not a difficult decision. "The French may display complete disregard for the welfare of those around them," Gilles Asselin and Ruth Mastron write. "In some cases, the need to *défendre son bifteck* (defend one's own steak) can be more important than high-flown notions of solidarity and unity" (2001, 19, 20).

French individualism *à l'extrême* was on display in a recent complaint lodged by Air France pilots against a company decision requiring them to speak English to ground controllers when landing at Charles de Gaulle airport in Paris. French pilots and controllers like to speak their mother tongue in these cases, but pilots from other countries complained that they couldn't understand exchanges between French pilots and the tower and that this posed a serious threat to safety. So Air France instituted an English-only policy, which was not well received by either pilots or controllers. Air France pilots know English, of course—"When they land in New York, they don't speak French," a company spokeswoman observed—but having to use such a barbarous tongue in their own national air-space is apparently too demeaning, even if that means endangering their own safety. After a ten-day trial period, Air France suspended the English-only policy (Swardson 2000).

The strong sense of self-pride among the French may stem from the relative lack of social and professional mobility in their society. Historically, one was born into one's station in life, and you were as likely to change it as you were to suddenly grow another arm. There was no notion of "doing something" with your life, as there was in America; you only resigned yourself to it. Unable to take any particular pride in what they have done, what they have made of their lives, the French cultivate instead an intense pride in who they are, in their personal identity. "Pride is very close to the self-esteem that has helped the European deal with his difficult world," Stuart Miller has observed.

> [I]n societies where life has been as hard as it has in Europe, the individual is driven to feed on the primal energy of his own individual existence and affirm it.
>
> Hence, the French peasant who has not enough money to buy even a horse, who has barely enough food to eat, can willfully assert his sense of personal being and worth.... This kind of defiance of circumstance and all other [people] is common in Europe.
>
> Because the European comes from a tradition much more closed to opportunity, the farmer, the working man, even the middle-class person, inherits centuries of institutionalized difficulty in social

mobility. Against the ceiling on his progress, he cultivates his pride in himself. (1990, 62, 63)

Their high self-regard also means that a French person's pride is never far below the surface and therefore quite vulnerable, which may account for the combative and self-protective streak in the French. They are alert to the smallest signs of disrespect from others, seeing slights or insults in the most innocuous behaviors, and are easily threatened, to which they respond with characteristic defensiveness. To some extent, the arrogance and superiority so often noted by foreigners may be nothing more than the French version of self-defense. The difference, of course, is the magnitude of the self to be defended.

Americans think of themselves as individualists, too, but their brand of individualism is nothing like the French variety. For Americans, being an individualist means being self-reliant and independent, able to look after yourself, and also having the freedom to say whatever you think. There is none of the French amour propre nor any sense that working with others somehow threatens individual freedom or self-respect. From the very beginning of the republic, Americans learned that if they didn't work together, they might very well perish—and would almost certainly not prosper. "During the formative period of American culture," John McElroy has written,

> to improve one's lot in life—and at times just to survive—demanded...forming organizations that would not only benefit the lives of individuals directly but also strengthen communities, and in that way indirectly benefit individuals.
>
> In places where few people live—such as a frontier or the rural communities and small towns that

replace a frontier—mutual reliance is as practical as self-reliance; and extending a helping hand to one's neighbor is no less important than taking responsibility for one's own well-being. (1999, 94, 95)

There is no room in such a scheme to let one's ego stand in the way of getting the job done, whether it's clearing the land and planting corn or keeping the assembly line running.

23. Religion and Politics

Americans and the French view the purpose of conversation quite differently, with the result that both the tone and the content of conversation likewise vary between the two cultures. For their part, the French like "meat" in their conversations. As Edward T. Hall and Mildred Reed Hall have noted, "The French relish conflict and spirited discussion" (1990, 102). The point of a conversation is not so much to have a pleasant exchange but to engage the other person in a lively, even heated debate about matters of substance. A good conversation, therefore, should be intellectually and emotionally stimulating; if it doesn't actually improve the mind, it should at least give it a vigorous workout. In short, the French take their conversations seriously and feel a duty to execute them as best they can, almost like an artist with a watercolor. Indeed, conversation is often referred to as an art in France (and on the continent in general). "In French we say that a conversation must be 'engaged,'" the French writer Raymonde Carroll has written,

> "sustained," "fueled," and "revived" if it is dragging, "rerouted" if it is dangerous. Once we permit a con-

versation to begin, we owe it to ourselves to keep it from dying, to care for it, to guide it, to watch over its development as if it were a living creature. (1988, 24)

There's a good chance that any conversation worthy of the name will eventually lead to disagreement, confrontation, and higher pulse rates. Indeed, people show their regard for the other people in a conversation [that they take them seriously] by being willing to challenge and attack their views and opinions. Anything less is almost disrespectful—and certainly not as much fun. To most Americans, a French conversation sounds exactly like an argument. "Americans tend to like people who agree with them," it has been has noted, whereas

French people are more likely to be interested in a person who disagrees with them.... A conversation where disagreements are exchanged [is] stimulating [to] a Frenchman, while an American is likely to be embarrassed. It is not uncommon to see two Frenchmen arguing with each other, their faces reddened with what seems to be anger, exchanging lively, heated and irreconcilable arguments. Then, later, they shake hands and [say], "That was a good discussion. Let's do it again sometime." (Harris and Moran 1987, 449)

The French recognize that there is such a thing as "polite" conversation, of course, where you talk about the weather and your dog, and they're quite good at it, but they don't enjoy it nearly as much as the real thing.

It's no wonder, then, that Pierre doesn't quite follow Suzanne's logic in the dialogue. She starts out by saying that discussing religion is dangerous, but when Pierre inquires as to the nature of the danger, the best Suzanne can manage is to say that people take religion seriously. To the French, for whom conversation is *supposed* to be serious, this is a non sequitur. Suzanne now tries again, explaining that friendships might be at stake here, but it turns out all she means by this is that there's a chance she and François might disagree during the course of their conversation, implying that disagreements can undermine friendships.

Suzanne's remarks get us closer to what may be the fundamental reason French and American conversations sound so different: the fact that the two cultures have different concepts of friendship. Simply stated, Americans seem to need their friends in a way the French do not. French people, like most Latins, tend to have strong ingroups, a tight circle of extended family members and one or two lifelong intimates (something more than what Americans call a friend) of whom one would not hesitate to ask anything and for whom one would likewise not hesitate to do anything. Such deep relationships cannot be threatened—and certainly not undone—by mere disagreements, which is why Pierre sees no risk in discussing serious subjects. "French friends do not seek to maintain harmony," Gilles Asselin and Ruth Mastron have observed,

> but rather to cultivate distinction and avoid boredom. They expect to disagree, to criticize, even to argue. A friend may be very direct, even frankly critical.... French people find it tedious to always be in agreement and for this reason may be attracted to friends who are quite different from themselves. Since the relationship is not based on agreement, it is not threatened by disagreement, and French

friends expect one another to comment honestly on their actions and choices. Support can be expressed in confrontation as well as by acquiescence. The bond between friends is not fragile and can stand up to this tension, even be strengthened and deepened by it. (2001, 89)

Perhaps because they move so much, Americans don't have ingroups in the way the French do. Or, if they do, then they consist only of immediate family members (and sometimes not even them). In any case, this means that Americans often have to rely on their friends in ways the French do not, turning to them, for example, for the kind of support the French would only ask of an ingroup member. Naturally, if you have to depend on your friends in times of need, then you would think twice about alienating them through confrontation or disagreement.

This is surely part of the reason, then, that American conversations are decidedly more slight and casual and not usually about anything too serious or significant, anything people might have strong feelings about. "Americans abide by a strong convention to preserve surface cordiality in social interactions," Edward Stewart and Milton Bennett have noted. "Kind words and pleasant smiles are natural and expected; sharp opinions and critical positions in face-to-face encounters are avoided for fear of disrupting social conviviality" (1991, 150). The American instinct, therefore, is to look for common ground in a conversation, to find a topic or position on which everyone can agree and to avoid topics on which they might not. Americans much prefer to "agree to disagree," as they say, rather than to actually disagree. If too much emotion starts to creep into the discussion, they are likely to change the subject to something more neutral. To this end they are taught at an early age to avoid two topics of conversation in particular, politics and religion, for these are subjects about which many people feel deeply. And deep feelings can too easily lead to emotional outbursts and confrontation. It's no wonder the French find American conversations frustratingly empty, or that Americans are frequently startled at the ferocity of French exchanges.

The American bias against too much talk may be another reason they don't do serious conversations very well. The United States is a country of doers, and talking, or at least that talking that is in lieu of doing, is suspect (see Dialogue 28, "The Thinker," page 107). The man and woman of action were always held in higher regard in America than thinkers and intellectuals. There are common expressions that denigrate talking and extol action; for example, "Put your money where your mouth is" and "Actions speak louder than words." Talking is a pleasant enough way to pass the time but not a serious pursuit or in and of itself significant; only when the talking stops does anything important happen.

The French, who love ideas and the life of the mind, naturally love conversation, for it is the primary arena in which one can display, promote, and defend one's ideas— and assert one's identity in the process. In many ways a French person's identity is in fact a combination of his or her ideas, opinions, and tastes. The books, music, and art one prefers (especially the *school* of each that one favors), the thinkers and intellectuals one agrees with, and most of all the political and social ideology one subscribes to— all of these are at the core of a Frenchman or -woman's sense of self. This is why only in France do you find such fierce arguments about whether this or that writer or composer really understands postmodernism, whether Sartre or Camus was the true existentialist, whether this or that politician is a real socialist. Conversation, those endless arguments in cafés and at dinner parties, is the lifeblood of the French. They can go without bread if they must, even wine, but they could not live without conversation.

24. Le Clos Is Late

The French have very few illusions—about life in general and about human nature in particular (though they suffer from the usual problem of seeing their *own* nature somewhat less objectively). Not to put too fine a face on it, they have a dim view of humanity and by and large do not believe in happy endings. If something can go wrong, it probably will, and, on the whole, other people can't be depended upon. Trust, in short, is a stranger to the French heart. "[In] general," Stuart Miller writes,

> the European exists in an inner world where things won't get better and life is not very good to begin with. Psychologically, this view shelters him from some of the shocks and disappointments of existence. Practically, such an attitude leads to the caution necessary for confronting what experience has shown to be a dangerous and intractable universe. (1990, 32)

It is the chronic Old World disease, pessimism, and it is never very far from the surface, as we see in this dialogue. Expecting the worst, as he instinctively does, Philippe doesn't hold out much hope for Le Clos, especially since there is already "a pattern here." But even if there weren't a pattern, even if Le Clos were a completely unknown entity, Philippe knows better than to be hopeful. That's just not how the world works.

Not his world, anyway. Marcia's world, on the other hand, has a very different cast. It's a positive place, practically teeming with optimism, where people have an almost innate faith in human nature (note the presumption of innocence in the American legal system). It's a world where people always give each other the benefit of the doubt ("I'm sure he's doing his best") and likewise take people at their word ("He told me how much this contract means to him"). It's a world where even in the face of a pattern, a bona fide reason to be pessimistic, Marcia still assumes the best about Le Clos. It's a world, in other words, where, ultimately, people can be trusted to do the right thing. It's also the reason Marcia probably finds Philippe cynical and defeatist, and the reason Philippe finds her hopelessly naive.

The French and the Americans come by their views of human nature quite honestly, of course, via their respective national experiences. Much of what the French have seen of humanity over the millennia has not been encouraging, and while France may have had its moments of hopefulness—surely the French Revolution was one—hope has never really prevailed. We might recall in this context that Voltaire's great hero Candide, he of the best of all possible worlds, was a comic figure.

The American national experience, hence the national outlook, has been considerably more positive. For most of its admittedly short history, the United States has known few wars on its own soil and suffered little from plagues or class struggles (though smallpox decimated several Native American tribes), and the country has been blessed with land that is both rich and abundant. American history has been a succession of victories and triumphs, whether over real enemies (the British, the Kaiser, Germany, and Japan) or over disease and poverty. To fare well in the U.S., all one has had to do was be willing to work hard. Under the circumstances, to be optimistic about life was simply a matter of believing in your own experience.

What has been called the immigrant mentality is no doubt another factor underlying the positive American outlook. In general, immigrants are people who don't accept life as they find it but strive to make it into something else. They are, accordingly, hopeful people, and they believe completely in themselves. It takes this kind of faith, after all, to prompt someone to leave behind all that is safe and certain and familiar and cast off for alien shores. Scratch the surface of an immigrant and one finds a person who refuses to resign him- or herself to the future but seeks to create it.

More than any other single factor, this tendency to be optimistic captures the essence of what was truly new about the New World. The landscape was different, of course, and the weather, the people, and hundreds of other particulars, but what was fundamentally different was the emotional and psychological mindset. Even today, nothing strikes Americans so strongly about Europeans as their air of resignation, their tendency to accept life more or less as they find it. This is an oversimplification, of course, and something which is no doubt changing with successive generations of Europeans, but the residue of fatalism still pervades European culture.

Meanwhile, the French shake their heads at American naiveté, as they see it, at American ignorance of the lessons of history (or at least of European history), which would give them the tragic sensibility so lacking in their culture. The French sociologist Michel Crozier has called optimism the "American disease." It is "America's essence," he says, "to be optimistically confident in the goodness of man, which was a stimulating attitude when the frontier was still open, but which is useless in coping with [the modern world]. America's disease is the result of not having enough sense of the evil in man" (in Zeldin 1996, 506).

25. Call Me Later

Americans and the French don't think about time in quite the same way. Indeed, they come from opposite sides of the great monochronic/polychronic divide, Edward Hall's famous paradigm that describes the different ways people around the world think about time and how their concept of time affects their relations with others.

The United States, home of the daily planner, is firmly in the monochronic camp, where time is seen as a commodity—a *limited* commodity—and where it therefore becomes important, nay vital, to use time as carefully as possible and to make the most of it. To this end monochronic types go to great lengths to manipulate and control time, imposing elaborate structures on it—schedules, deadlines, flow charts, time lines, time frames—and then organize their lives around these structures. As these structures become dominant, people become subordinate, so that in monochronic cultures, people adjust to the demands of time and schedules, but time and schedules are rarely adjusted to suit the needs of people. If you call when someone is in a meeting, for example, you will almost surely be told to call back. No one would think of stopping the meeting, for this would mean disrupting the structure. Needless to say, spontaneous, accidental, or otherwise unplanned occurrences wreak havoc in a monochronic world, for by definition they take place outside the structure and cannot easily be accommodated. They are all varieties of interruption, and interruptions are the bane of a monochronic person's life. There is, of course, a touching irony at the heart of the monochronic worldview: in going to such lengths to subdue and control time, monochronic types end up being dominated by it.

Two other features of monochronic cultures are that people tend to do things one at a time and to feel that they can talk or otherwise give attention to only one other person at a time. Parents in monochronic cultures, for example, are known for telling small children that they can't talk to "Mommy right now because Mommy is talking to Daddy." This preference for dealing with people one at a time is the reason everyone lines up in monochronic cultures, for lines only make sense, of course, if people expect to be waited on one at a time.

In a polychronic world, it is people who push time around, not vice versa. Time is not regarded as a commodity, so there is not this urgency about time, hence about life. Nor is there the corresponding urge to control or manipulate time or to devise systems and structures to maximize its use. People come first in polychronic cultures, and time is their servant. There is always more time, and people are never too busy to see you. It's not that such people don't have schedules and deadlines, but only that they are neither dominated nor intimidated by them. A meeting might very well be stopped while a participant takes a telephone call, or an appointment might be changed at the last minute. What monochronic types call interruptions, polychronic types call life.

Which brings us, finally, to Carl (in the dialogue), who has dropped by his old friend Jean Paul's office on the chance Jean Paul might be "free." Coming from a mono-chronic culture, Carl operates under the assumption that his spontaneous, unplanned visit to Jean Paul's office may be inconvenient, that Jean Paul might have something scheduled. And when it turns out Jean Paul does, then Carl's visit (from his perspective) suddenly turns into an interruption, which he immediately tries to minimize by beating a hasty retreat.

Carl's behavior must be very puzzling to the polychronic Jean Paul, who may indeed keep a schedule but who is not at all inconvenienced by this unexpected development and would have no trouble incorporating Carl into his morn-ing. What he would do, in fact, is simply turn his meeting with one person, La Roche, into a meeting with two, Carl and La Roche, and the polychronic La Roche would un-derstand. Jean Paul also has to be wondering why Carl doesn't seize the opportunity to learn more about the BDM negotiations and especially why Carl asks him to call later, when they have the chance to talk right now, face-to-face. For Carl to have to come back later, when he's right here—now *that* would be inconvenient.

Jean Paul tries to deal with reality—Carl is here, after all—and for reality, he will make adjustments. Carl, on the other hand, tries to change the reality and simply not be there. In the end what the monochronic Carl doesn't understand is that the polychronic Jean Pauls of the world are always free, for they have never been imprisoned in the first place.

26. At the Window

This dialogue features more fallout from the power dis-tance and amour propre concepts discussed earlier, with a coda addressing the fate of the customer in France. There are two important things to know about power in France: it is the key to success and advancement, and it is widely believed to exist in limited amounts. The competition for power, in all its forms, therefore, is naturally quite intense. In France, as in most countries, power often comes in the form of information, which means that anything to do with getting and holding on to information is serious business. In this context, it's no wonder the notion of keeping people "in the loop" has never quite caught on in France (though information networks, curiously enough, are well developed and much cultivated). Indeed, the whole idea is to keep other people *out* of the loop as much as possible. When I know something you don't, I have the upper hand, and getting the upper hand is the name of the game in high power-distance France. The French, don't forget, have a hard time trusting other people—they trust their subordinates least of all—and tend to look upon power as a kind of protection against those who would try to replace them. In many companies even deputies, those who must be ready to step in and take over at a moment's notice, are not kept informed for fear of giving them too much of an advantage. "At all levels of society," Michel Crozier has written, "the French, once they gain entry into an influential group, instinctively try to keep others out" (in Hill 1994, 53).

Managers, such as the supervisors referred to by Carol in the dialogue, are in the forefront of power struggles, and they use whatever means they can to assert and protect their interests. If on occasion this should mean not sharing information with subordinates—tellers, for example—then so be it. "Getting a group of French people to work together virtually defies the laws of dynamics," Richard Hill has observed in his book *WeEuropeans*. "Each

of them runs his or her own little fiefdom and the operat-
ing principle (from the top down, which is the only way
French business works) appears to be management by information retention" (1995, 70).

Which brings us to Michelle, the supervisor in the dialogue, who has just been told by a very excited Carol ("I
have some great news") that some software she has tracked
down promises to deliver to tellers information heretofore
only available to supervisors. For the Michelles of the
world, who regard information roughly the way a dog regards a bone, the day is getting off to a very poor start.

You might think Michelle would at least be happy in
the sense that the new procedure is certainly going to be
very good for business. And what's good for business is good
for everybody. But if you think like that, then chances are
you're not French. The French tend not to think in terms
of the enterprise as a whole, what Americans call the "big
picture," or of what's good for everybody; they worry, rather,
about their own particular piece of the enterprise and what's
good for them. Let others, senior management, for example,
worry about the big picture; that's what they get paid for.
In her heart of hearts, Michelle probably knows she's being shortsighted, that pulling together for the common
good is simply good business sense, but the common good
is just too much of an abstraction for the highly individualist French to identify with. They can't quite grasp it.

"In the contextual ethics of the French," it has been
noted,

> practical self-interest is important, and they tend
> to admire someone who can gain an advantage in
> a situation. The American notion of a level play-
> ing field tends not to resonate with the French,

who generally feel that a person should make use
of every possible advantage. Self-interest must be
served.... (Asselin and Mastron 2001, 17)

Be that as it may, you say to yourself, surely Michelle
can at least muster some excitement for the customer, who
stands to benefit greatly from the increased efficiency of
the new arrangement. But you would be wrong again. For
one thing, this isn't really about efficiency; it's about power.
For another, it turns out that the customer doesn't reign
quite so supreme in France as in many other countries.
The French have nothing against the customer, of course,
not most of the time, anyway, but the customer doesn't
always come first in France and, furthermore, is not necessarily always right (as the customer is said to be in the
United States). "The plight of the customer is desperate
[in France]," Polly Platt has written, referring to the treatment of customers in supermarkets and department stores.
"Work places are about giving employment, not service....
Customers are a nuisance" (1995, 72).

This is our old friend amour propre again, the high
self-regard that makes it so difficult for the French to put
the interests of someone else ahead of their own. One could
always nitpick, of course, and point out that if one is in
the business of customer service, then the interests of others are the same as his or her own, but that would be too
practical. "In French eyes," Hill observes, "putting oneself
readily at the disposal of a total stranger is an affront to
one's self-esteem: like the Spanish, the French have difficulty in recognizing the difference between service and
servility" (1994, 59). The long history of feudalism all but
guarantees that the French would be especially sensitive
to the notion of "serving" someone else and would be likely

to err on the side of neglect. To which one hastens to add the standard warning that context is everything; in small neighborhood shops, for example, where the customer is known, employees go out of their way to be helpful.

Compared with the French, Americans are somewhat uncomfortable with power (see Dialogue 19, "Bothering the Chief," page 102), and the best bosses are those who wear their power lightly. Companies strive constantly to become "flatter" organizations and to create maximum autonomy for workers. The deep egalitarian strain in American culture leaves no room for autocrats; bosses who flaunt their power may have to be "cut down to size," as Americans put it, or have perhaps "forgotten where they came from." Nor is power regarded as an end in itself, as it is in France, as something to acquire almost for its own sake, or if not quite for its own sake, then mainly to intimidate others. In the United States power is merely a means to an end, the end being to guarantee the success of the enterprise, not simply to hold on to one's power. In France bosses are respected largely because of their power; in the U.S., bosses have power only if they are respected. "In egalitarian American culture," Gilles Asselin and Ruth Mastron observe,

> power is almost a dirty word, and while people acknowledge the existence of office politics, they regard such maneuvering as slightly distasteful. Companies talk of the participative workplace where employees are empowered to control their own jobs and destinies. The idea of having power over someone, or, worse yet, being under someone's power, makes most Americans vaguely uncomfortable.....
> In France and other Latin cultures, power is acknowledged and spoken of openly. High-level

people use their power freely, usually to their own advantage, and are respectfully deferred to by those they control. (2001, 200)

In the United States the customer is still king—and virtually an emperor compared with the customer in France. The American worker has no trouble thinking beyond his or her own good to the good of the enterprise, hence the customer. Nor do Americans wrestle with servility the way the French do; in a culture founded on the concept of equality, customers instinctively know better than to act superior.

27. Lunch with Gallimard

Numerous observers have described a deep Latin strain in French culture, referring to the fact that the French exhibit a number of characteristics normally identified with people from countries of southern Europe and the Mediterranean. This is important for Americans, who are used to some of the common cultural differences of the northern-tier European countries but will not necessarily be prepared for the degree and kind of difference they may encounter in France. If they have had dealings with the Spanish or the Italians, for example, they may be less surprised by some of the behaviors of the French than if they have worked only with Germans, say, or Scandinavians. For their part, the French need to keep in mind that they often present a far more foreign face to Americans than do most other northern Europeans.

We have already examined a number of these Latin-like characteristics in earlier dialogues—the tendency to be polychronic, the high power-distance mentality, the ingroup/outgroup orientation—and this dialogue presents another: the importance of establishing personal relationships with people before entering into business arrangements with them. For the French, the deciding factor in a business partnership will not necessarily be the terms of the deal—price, quality, features, availability—but how strong a personal relationship the partners can forge. Is there trust? Is there rapport? Doing business together, after all, is almost like a marriage—an intense, lifelong relationship with numerous ups and downs—and you want to choose your partner carefully. If a relationship can be established, then the terms can always be worked out—what are terms between friends?—but if there is no rapport or trust, then the terms won't matter in the end.

Ideally, of course, a French entrepreneur prefers to do business only with members of his or her ingroup, with people with whom one already has the strongest possible relationship. But that's not always realistic. Second best, then, would be to have as your partner a friend or acquaintance or relative of someone in your ingroup; you may not know this person, but someone you know and trust does, someone who would never lead you astray. Even then, you would have to forge your own personal bond with this individual, but you have a head start because of your mutual acquaintance.

Where neither of these two options is available—where a personal bond does not already exist (members of your ingroup) or cannot be presumed (friends of friends, someone you were at the *grande école* with)—then that bond has to be created, and that is the whole purpose of the upcoming lunch with Gallimard (at least in Marcel's mind). It will be a chance for Joyce and Gallimard to meet and begin laying the foundation for a relationship. Chances are they won't get around to business at this meeting, but that's not the point. There's no rush, after all, since this relationship could very well last for years; indeed, it is precisely *because* it may last for years that both parties should take their time.

"Wining and dining are more important the further south one goes in Europe," John Mole has observed,

> not because southerners are more sybaritic but because of different concepts of the role of personal relationships within a business relationship. In northern Europe and even more so in North America a business relationship is seen as independent from a personal relationship. It is possible to walk into the office of a complete stranger with a proposal and begin to talk business. The further south you go in Europe…the more important it is to cement social and personal relationships before you can even start to work together…. Potential partners look for reassurance that they are good people to do business with before they look at the deal itself. (1995, 192, 193)

The upcoming lunch, in short, will be a lengthy affair, as both parties try to get a feeling for the other person and some sense of whether or not there's any basis for a business relationship. This will certainly be Gallimard's expectation—why else would you have lunch with perfect strangers?—and also explains why Marcel suggests rescheduling the lunch when he learns Joyce has allowed a mere ninety minutes for this event. Ninety minutes will seem very rushed, hence rude, to Gallimard—it defeats the purpose, in fact—which is why Marcel wants to reschedule the lunch to a time when it can unfold more leisurely.

Edward T. and Mildred Reed Hall have pointed out that
the average business lunch in France lasts 124 minutes compared with an average of 64 minutes in the United States
(1990, 120). We should also note, for the record, that we
are talking about lunch here, the most important meal of
the day, about which the French take their time. Business
or no business, the French don't rush lunch—or anything
else to do with food.

Joyce doesn't see things quite this way. In her world
finding a business partner is largely a matter of shopping
around for the best deal. Most people are reliable, after all,
and if they turn out not to be, you just keep trying until
you find someone who is. In any event business relationships don't usually endure. They are opportunistic and usually last only as long as they continue to serve the interests
of both parties; when either of the parties finds a better
opportunity elsewhere, the relationship ends, generally
without any hard feelings.

For this very reason Americans, unlike the French, actually try to avoid doing business with close friends or family
members. Business can be quite cutthroat, after all, and if
you have to cut another person's throat, it's easier if it's
someone you're not especially close to. This is not to say
that it doesn't matter to Americans whether they have
rapport with or can trust the people with whom they do
business; it means only that as a rule Americans don't select business partners *primarily* on that basis. In "the United
States," it has been observed, "the business drives the relationship, while in France, the relationship usually drives
the business" (Asselin and Mastron 2001, 180).

When Joyce meets Gallimard, then, her agenda is quite
simple: after the initial pleasantries, they will get down to
business. If there is a meeting of the minds, they may ar-

range to talk further; if there isn't, no harm has been done. Whatever happens, it's not going to take that long; ninety minutes should be more than enough. As for the fact that it's lunch, to Americans the operative word in the phrase "business lunch" is business, not lunch.

28. The Thinker

The French love ideas and everything associated with ideas: philosophy and philosophers, of course, but also books of any kind (*Apostrophes*, one of the most popular TV shows in France, is all about the latest books), serious conversation, and anything else that comes under the general heading of "intellectual." It was a Frenchman, after all, the great Descartes, who said "I think; therefore, I am," and another French philosopher, Pascal, who defined man as *un roseau pensant*, a thinking reed. Being an intellectual comes closer to an actual profession in France than in practically any other country, and one of the greatest compliments you can pay a French person is to call him or her an intellectual. As Lynn Payer has written, "One must understand that the French, more than just about any other nationality, value thinking as an activity in itself" (1989, 37). Payer's point is well taken, for while many cultures value ideas and thinking, very few value them for their own sake the way the French seem to. "The French are doomed to be abstract," D. H. Lawrence wrote. "Talking to them is like trying to have a relationship with the letter 'x' in algebra" (in Hill 1995, 78).

   This does not make the French very good at actually getting things done. Indeed, as soon as an idea begins to migrate away from being a concept toward some kind of actual application, away from the abstract toward the more concrete, the French lose interest. After all, what is a sordid and imperfect application next to a beautiful theory? Delivering on their wonderful concepts, in other words, just doesn't engage the French quite as much as formulating them in the first place. Analysis, discussion, theorizing of any kind—these intrigue the French greatly; implementation merely bores them. "Implementation is not a French strength," Peter Lawrence and Vincent Edwards have observed. "[I]t is an unprogrammable, messy, hands-on, compromise-driven enterprise best delegated to somebody more junior" (2000, 44).

When a French company has a vacancy to fill, especially in management, it wants a thinker, not the so-called "people person" Americans often recruit. "People who run big enterprises must above all else be clever," Jean-Louis Barsoux and Peter Lawrence have written.

> The emphasis on cleverness shows up even in executive recruiting advertisements. They hardly mention the drive or initiative looked for in Anglo-Saxon recruits; rather they call for more cerebral qualities—an analytical mind, independence, intellectual rigor , an ability to synthesize information. Communication or interpersonal skills are tacked on at the end, if they appear at all. (1991, 60)

Americans are another breed entirely. For the most part, they have no particular interest in ideas nor in abstract things in general—and no interest whatsoever in ideas for their own sake. The pragmatic streak runs so deep in the national psyche that anything that is not patently utilitarian is almost automatically suspect. Thus, you will get an American's attention if you show him or her the practical application of an idea or how to make money from it, but otherwise ideas have very little legitimacy. And as for being an intellectual, it's something you might whisper to trusted comrades, but it is nothing like the badge of honor it is in France. Indeed, Americans are unapologetically anti-intellectual. How else to explain the dismissive tone toward academia in the United States, and especially toward academics, the much-maligned denizens of the Ivory Tower whose only real failing seems to be that they don't *do* anything—except, of course, think and write? The U.S., we should not forget, is the country where "those who can, do," and where "those who can't, teach." Is it any wonder, then, that there has never been a great American philosopher, except perhaps for William James whose contribution to the field was the theory of pragmatism!

It's no surprise, then, that Todd and Gerard view their colleague Henri differently. Gerard values his great mind and stimulating conversation ("His ideas are really wonderful") and sees these as tremendous assets to the organization. The more practical Todd regards Henri's inability to produce on schedule as a serious liability. Needless to say, Gerard can't imagine why Todd would have complained to M. Cardin ("You've complained? Why?").

As noted earlier (Dialogue 23, "Religion and Politics," page 104), their love of "doing" also makes Americans wary and suspicious of talk, and especially of talk that is a substitute for or that gets in the way of action. This is why Todd cuts Gerard off when Gerard starts to describe the "great talk" he and Henri had had the previous day. Whatever those two talked about, it didn't put Henri any closer to his deadline. And that's what matters.

This love of ideas is not merely indulgence or escape on the part of the French; it is, rather, part of a deeper and quite legitimate compulsion: the pursuit of truth. If the French sometimes get carried away by their passion for ideas, in other words, one is not to worry; it's all for a good cause. Sanche de Gramont has observed that the French

> want to organize the universe; better a wrong theory than no theory. Everything must be labeled and classified. This is what one might call "the determination to shatter the charm." Mystery cannot be tolerated; it must be broken down into its component parts.... [The French assume] the laws of nature can be discerned by the correct application of reason. The supremacy of reason is hammered into the French consciousness at an early age. The English child is told be "be good" (stressing character), but the French child is asked to "be reasonable" (*sois raisonnable*). He will continue, as a result of his schooling, to favor theoretical hypotheses that lead to abstract conclusions. (1969, 315)

As noted earlier, Americans were more or less obliged by circumstances to be doers. It wasn't that they had anything *against* thinking; they were just too busy to pay it any heed. Thinking, after all, is a luxury for those who have already created their country, but in the New World there wasn't time for thinking; indeed, there was barely time for all the doing that had to be done. "[T]he need to master the wilderness and extract its natural resources," Richard Pells has noted,

> to construct great cities and develop a modern industrial nation, had required a practical, problem-solving cast of mind. Consequently, Americans preferred the "man of action" to the theorist, the

person who rejected absolutes in favor of concrete solutions that worked in the particular instance. The classic American hero was the inventor, the engineer, the technological wizard, not the artist or academic. (1997, 178, 179)

There may be an even deeper strain of the American character at work here, and that is the deep-seated faith in empiricism, in accepting as true and real only that which has been personally experienced. The only ideas that matter, that can be truly relied upon and trusted, are those that have come from the school of life. And the only philosophers who dispense such ideas are those with practical experience, men and women of action. Intellectuals, in short, need not apply. "[T]he person who discovered something in the 'school of hard knocks' through hands-on learning," John McElroy has observed, "or who created something new and useful as a result of what he had learned on his own by trial-and-error experimentation or independent study, was more greatly respected and admired than the man of book learning" (1999, 102).

Naturally, the French tend to find Americans intellectual lightweights and have trouble taking them seriously, even as Americans believe the French think too much and are wildly impractical. Even so, one can't help but sense a certain reluctant admiration beneath French disdain for American anti-intellectualism. They would never say so, but they secretly envy the dynamism of Americans, although it leaves them quite breathless at times, and they occasionally dream of what great heights might be scaled if only American energy could be harnessed to the service of first-rate French ideas.

29. Mistakes

To err may indeed be human, but you would never know it by observing the French. Simply put, the French do not err—or, more accurately, they never admit to having made an error and will go to great, even comic, lengths to avoid blame or criticism in any form. Polly Platt once saw a Frenchwoman in a fancy tearoom get up from her table "with a swirl of her cape, which threw the sugar bowl to the floor. Sugar cubes scattered far and wide. 'What a stupid place to put a sugar bowl,' she said huffily." On another occasion, a French guest at Platt's house spilled a glass of red wine on her beige sofa. "'What a strange color for a sofa!' was her only comment" (1995, 84).

In the dialogue the American, Darryl, has unknowingly put Jean Claude on the defensive by using the dreaded word *mistakes*. While the typical American response to charges of mistakes would be to look into the matter and get to the bottom of it, the typical French reaction is to deny everything and immediately go on the offensive—to escape blame at all costs, which is just what Jean Claude does when he asks, "Andre? How did he get involved?" He completely sidesteps the charges themselves and attacks his attacker.

For his part Darryl finds Jean Claude's question beside the point—what does it matter how Andre or anyone else got involved?—and simply ignores it ("I have no idea"), asking instead to see the spec sheet. This only puzzles Jean Claude further, of course ("You want to see it?"), since he hasn't really grasped why Darryl insists on giving credence to this preposterous notion of mistakes. He tries one last time to steer Darryl in the right direction, to see that Andre is the problem ("Andre must be upset about something"), but Darryl doesn't get it. ("Yeah," Darryl answers. "The specs!")

Why are the French so afraid to admit mistakes or reveal weakness? One likely explanation is the amour propre, or exceptionally high self-regard, described back in Dialogue 22 ("Withholding," pages 103–104). The high opinion the French have of themselves doesn't leave much room for self-doubt or self-criticism, and their personal pride likewise guarantees that any mistakes the French might acknowledge inwardly would never be made known to others. It's simply not in character, in short, for people with so much invested in their self-esteem to acknowledge incompetence or confess to any kind of ignorance or carelessness.

Another, even more compelling explanation for this tendency is the deep-seated, instinctive distrust the French have of other people. The French have a dim view of the great mass of humanity and are quite sure they're up to no good. If the world really is full of people who are out to take advantage of you, and if, beyond that, the world is so constructed that others can only succeed if you fail—then you might as well hand your head to other people on a platter as admit to a mistake. As noted earlier, the French believe that only so many opportunities present themselves as one goes through life and that even to *get* an opportunity, regardless of what is done with it, is extremely rare. Under the circumstances, to admit failure—to acknowledge *squandering* an opportunity—takes considerable courage.

"The American has a tradition of entitlement to multiple lives, to forgiveness and new starts," Stuart Miller has observed.

Not in Europe. There, instead, everyone keeps comprehensive files on everyone else. One chance is all you get.... Personal weaknesses and wrongs are [remembered], everything is carried on the books. True, it is not as bad as it once was, when the peccadilloes or sins of a single member could for generations cast doubt on the worth of the whole family. Nevertheless, the European is further driven to conceal himself from others because everything he does reveal will be taken down and for many years may be used in evidence against him; and he is further pushed to be distrustful because he knows others are engaging in the same maneuvers of concealment as he. (1990, 42, 43)

Americans, as Miller notes, live in a much more forgiving world. By and large they do not feel that other people are out to get them, and their experience has taught them that there is enough opportunity for everyone to succeed. In such a benign universe, there is no shame in failure and no risk in admitting error. Indeed, the only shame is in not trying in the first place.

Beyond that, Americans, from the beginning of the republic, have been on a never-ending quest for self-improvement. The opportunity to make something better of their lives was what brought immigrants here in the first place, and personal as well as national improvement has been a consistent theme in American history. Whatever one achieves, one can always achieve more, and however much one has bettered oneself—socially, personally, educationally—one can always add even to that. In such a scheme, admitting one's mistakes and shortcomings is merely how people learn and grow; how they discover what they don't know, for example, and still need to learn; how they uncover flaws in a product or process and then perfect it; and how they identify their personal weaknesses and overcome them. "In the United States," one executive has observed, "admitting error is not only seen as honest, but important. You're not perceived as learning much if you don't make mistakes" (Platt 1995, 222).

The American penchant for admitting mistakes, the confessional mode Americans can so easily fall into, is not seen by the French the way Americans see it (as a necessary precondition for self-improvement) but as needlessly exposing their weaknesses to those who would take advantage. "Americans tell everything about themselves," one observer has noted, "and even insist on the disagreeable aspects of their country, which others would conceal: statistics on crime, reports on juvenile delinquency, full accounts of any immoral act whatever." The obsessiveness with which the United States disclosed its shortcomings prompted one observer to declare that there was "no anti-Americanism as eloquent as that of Americans [themselves]" (Pells 1997, 173).

In dealing with the French, Americans have to be careful how they raise the subject of mistakes. "The thing to do is to tell [them] indirectly," an American expat advises. "'I think there is something wrong here,' you say pleasantly. No accusations. No stern tone. Then [they'll] look it over and be very proud of finding 'an error.' Accusing [them] will bring an explosion of denials and possibly unpleasantness" (Platt, 222).

30. Running Late

This dialogue features more fallout from the clash of monochronic and polychronic worldviews discussed in Dialogue

25 ("Call Me Later," page 105). In the present example, the two features of this cultural difference on display are being late and allowing for interruptions. In both mono-chronic and polychronic cultures, being late and thereby keeping someone waiting is considered rude and unpro-fessional, and the longer one is kept waiting, the greater the slight. Being made to wait (at least without an expla-nation) says either that your business is not important (and this is how the other person is signaling you) or that it is not *as* important as whatever business the person making you wait is doing instead. This is what has caused Janet to conclude that her business must pale in comparison with the marketing director's ("Must be really important, eh?").

But she has misinterpreted the situation. In polychronic France, M. LeBlanc isn't even late yet, nor is Janet twenty minutes into her wait as she seems to think. Strictly speak-ing, waiting can't begin until the other person is "late" for an appointment, and "late" is entirely a function of how a particular culture defines lateness. Polychronic cultures define it much more loosely than do monochronic ones, depending on the circumstances. In the United States a person is late for an appointment roughly ten minutes af-ter the specified meeting time. We know this because in such situations the offending party will invariably apolo-gize or offer an explanation for what has caused the delay. But the French are more casual about appointments and often do not consider a person (or themselves) late until half an hour has elapsed. Depending on the situation, no explanation may be called for or expected. This is why Claude doesn't understand ("How do you mean?") when Janet says the marketing director's business "must be re-ally important."

The other difference illustrated in the dialogue is how monochronic and polychronic cultures define interruptions. As noted earlier, monochronic types prefer never to do more than one thing at a time and to give their undivided attention to that task or person. Polychronic people, however, frequently attend to several things simultaneously and can split their attention as necessary. Technically, then, a polychronic person *can't* be interrupted; that is, someone not in the habit of focusing exclusively on one thing at a time does not experience the sudden arrival of a second thing or person as a distraction. "The world of polychronics is abuzz with people," Polly Platt has written, referring to the French.

> The more people around all the time, the better; the more things happening at once, the better. Appointments are for giving a general idea; they're easily postponed or canceled, and not necessarily exclusive. Others may be booked into the same slot, which is probably open-ended, or they may simply occupy it jointly without warning. Polychronics can listen to three conversations at the same time and also take someone's pulse, sign a document, or fill out an airplane ticket. (1995, 51)

Hence, Claude's suggestion to take Janet into LeBlanc's office ("I can show you in if you like") while he is still meeting with his marketing director would most likely not interrupt the two men; it would only cause them to redistribute their attention. And it would, incidentally, mean that LeBlanc was no longer keeping Janet waiting!

French casualness about time (as Americans see it) earns them the reputation of being unprofessional or at least unreliable, of not taking business seriously. It may also add to the image of French arrogance; they come when they please, offering no excuses or apologies, exhibiting that characteristic French disdain for the feelings of others. For their part the French find monochronic types to be unhealthily obsessed with time and schedules and surprisingly insensitive to circumstances. Indeed, the French willingness to chuck schedules aside when necessary—to spend a little longer talking with the marketing director, for example, so he doesn't have to come back later—marks *theirs* as the culture that is truly concerned for the feelings of others.

31. Sales Figures

Americans tend to be an impatient and impulsive lot. Rather than let nature take its course, their instinct is to take hold of nature and determine its course. And the American attitude toward the future is likewise not so much that one waits for it to happen but that one shapes or even creates it. This may all be an illusion, of course, in the sense that Americans only imagine that events have responded to their manipulation, but it is a deep-seated illusion and one that keeps many researchers and scientists gainfully employed.

This interventionist, activist approach to life creates a certain sense of urgency, the expectation that things will happen in a timely fashion. This in turn is at least partly responsible for the short-term outlook that is typical of many Americans. Because there is always something they can *do* about a situation, a way of producing a desired response, there is no need to wait and see what happens. If the hoped-for result doesn't appear likely, then they intervene and *make* it happen. Businessmen or -women don't *wait* for sales figures, at least not for very long; they create them.

This explains Peter's eagerness in the dialogue. We are two quarters, six entire months, into the life of this product, plenty of time to judge its appeal and make necessary adjustments. He has, of course, misunderstood Brigitte's remarks about "two quarters," which to European sensibilities (see below) is no time at all. Indeed, the product may not have even arrived in some markets yet, much less had judgment passed upon it. These things take time; people need to get used to a product, to try it in different circumstances, compare it with competing products, talk about it with other people, and see if it holds up over the long run. Making changes too soon only confuses people or, worse, suggests a lack of confidence in the product. The idea that the company would make changes after two quarters, that market share could be *gained* in such a short time, to say nothing about lost, is quite foreign to Brigitte.

What explains the proactive mentality of the typical American? For one thing, the United States is a young culture, and young cultures, like young people, tend to be impatient. They don't realize—or, more accurately, they don't accept—that certain things take time. They *can* take time, no doubt, but do they really have to? Time is also quite relative; for young people, a month can seem like forever, whereas for older people, a year, even five years, is not so long in the grand scheme of things. Americans are used to things happening fast, to constant progress and rapid change; the latest gadget, discovery, or fad is obsolete, in some cases, before many people have even heard of it. When a new product goes on the market, no doubt its much-improved successor already exists as a prototype in someone's lab. "I accost an American sailor," Alexis de Tocqueville writes, "and inquire why the ships in his country are built to last such a short time; he answers, without hesitation, that the art of navigation is every day making such rapid progress that the finest vessel would become almost useless if it lasted beyond a few years" (1984, 158). America is a country, after all, which in just over three and a half centuries went from a wilderness to a superpower and the most technologically advanced society on earth. Americans aren't used to waiting for things to happen.

In a sense, however, the questions still remain: Why is American life so fast paced? Why aren't Americans used to waiting? Ultimately the answer may lie in the concept of locus of control introduced in the preceding chapter (Dialogue 7, "All the Stops," page 26). As many observers have pointed out, the people who came to the New World believed in themselves and, most especially, in their ability to make things happen. Their experience, from the moment of their arrival, only confirmed their faith. Whatever they tried, they almost always succeeded, and the habit of success, of continuous improvement in their circumstances, reinforced their belief in their ability to determine their own destiny. For Americans, then, the locus of control is internal; circumstances will always respond to the actions of individuals or groups of individuals. There are no givens, no situations or conditions that must be accepted as they are and that cannot be influenced or changed. If the public isn't responding the way one wants it to, then one simply does something about it, after a decent interval, of course. The discussion, incidentally, is never about *whether* anything can be done, but only about *what* must be done.

Older cultures, like France, are more humble. Their history has taught them that some things can't be changed and must be accepted as they are. Accordingly, the French assign humankind a lesser, more modest role in shaping events and unfolding the future. Individuals can and should exert their influence, of course, and will no doubt achieve results, but they are not the only players in the game. There are fate, or destiny, external circumstances, God—and all of them have their part to play as well and are quite beyond human control or influence. The locus of control for the French, in other words, is only partly internal.

While Europeans in general are more fatalistic than Americans are, the French are more so than all other northern Europeans. One way this is manifested, as in the dialogue, is in a willingness to let events take their course once they have been set in motion, after doing everything possible, of course. This view of human affairs tends to make the French a more patient, less driven people, and very much inclined to a long-term outlook. Things take time; people do what they can and then wait to see what happens next. Americans aren't interested in *seeing* what happens next; they mean to determine what happens next.

32. Madame X
33. Dinner on Friday
34. Meeting Jeanette

These three dialogues all deal with the issue of personal privacy and the larger question of interpersonal relations. They illustrate key differences in the way Americans and the French conceive of and interact with people they don't know ("Madame X" and "Meeting Jeanette") or people outside of their inner circle ("Dinner on Friday"). By and large, the French (and most Europeans) are much more private than are Americans, observing a much greater emotional and psychological distance between themselves and others than is the case in the United States. The French assume other people want to be left alone, and they rarely speak to, make eye contact with, or otherwise intrude on people they don't know. The French public face is closed, in short, and the French believe that access to another person should be granted, not assumed.

This attitude owes a lot to the ingroup/outgroup mentality described elsewhere in these pages, the notion that except for immediate family and a handful of lifelong friends, everyone belongs to one's outgroup, the great mass of humanity toward whom one has no obligations or responsibilities and who recognize none in return. "The basic social arrangement in France," Jean-Louis Barsoux and Peter Lawrence have written, "is the circle—a person is responsible only to people in his own *cercle* and indifferent to people outside it. French dislike for people outside their own *cercle* is epitomized by Sartre's phrase, '*l'enfer c'est les autres*' ('Hell is other people'—*Huis clos*, scene V)" (1997, 116).

Americans tend to be much less guarded than the French around people they don't know, regarding strangers more as friends they have not yet met. In the United States, in short, other people are not nearly as "other" as they are in France, and the American public face, accordingly, is decidedly more open. Where the French are inclined toward self-protection, Americans seem to delight in self-revelation. In their book, *Au Contraire! Figuring Out the French*, Gilles Asselin and Ruth Mastron describe what they call French

"psychological privacy," the need to keep things to oneself, or a tendency not to open up.... There sometimes seems to be a wall around peoples' private lives, the height of which varies according to the person they meet.

French people learn early on that personal information should not be revealed to just anyone and that a certain degree of intimacy must be reached before a person can open up. The amount of private information French people deliver in public is therefore much less than in the United States.

As an example, compare the behavior of people sitting next to each other on domestic flights in France and the U.S. In France—and in fact in most of Europe—people sitting next to each other rarely speak and rapidly find a book to read or another "safe" occupation that maintains the psychological wall around them.... Americans, on the other hand, are much more inclined to strike up a friendly conversation with seatmates, sometimes getting into relatively personal subjects. (2001, 54–55)

Among Europeans, Americans are notorious for their openness, for the ease and speed with which they grant relative strangers access to their lives and their homes. All this is not to say, incidentally, that Americans are friendly and considerate toward others and the French are cold and reserved; it merely means that both the Americans and the French are friendly and considerate—in very different ways.

In the first of the three dialogues, Ann assumes that her friend Alain will know something about a woman they encounter in the elevator of Alain's apartment building. After all, Madame X and Alain both live in the same building, which already makes them something more than strangers, and Alain even says he sees her in the elevator almost every day. So naturally Ann assumes he will know her name.

But Alain doesn't know, of course, for he is French, and the fact that he bumps into someone on an elevator almost every day, an entirely random affair, after all, hardly makes the two of them friends. To actively engage her in conversation would be seen as impolite, as pushing oneself upon others. "It is only by chance that we live so close to each other," Raymonde Carroll says of the other tenants in her apartment building,

> and this is not a sufficient reason for us to develop a relationship, unless of course, we specifically choose to do so. Similarly, on a small, quiet, provincial street it suffices for me to nod my head and to say hello to the neighbors who live next door and across the street (unless an extraordinary event interrupts the routine).
>
> In the absence of any relationship, silence is [normal].... This is why in the elevator, in the street, on the bus, and in practically every place where the other is almost totally foreign to my daily life, where the context does not call for ties to be formed, people don't talk to each other.... (1988, 27, 30)

In effect the French regard chance encounters as if they have not occurred, as if the other person is not actually there, for clearly that is how each party wants to be treated. This is why the French don't smile or make eye contact on the street, for example, and why Alain and Madame X have respected each other's deep desire for privacy on all of those occasions when they have met, exchanging little more than "Bonjour" and polite nods. They are strangers, in short, and in France one doesn't ask strangers their name. (One important exception to this rule would be in those instances where the stranger or unknown person dropped something, say, or was lost or otherwise in difficulty, in which case the French are extremely solicitous, more so in fact than are Americans.)

Americans don't necessarily bond for life with people they meet on elevators either, of course, but even so, for most Americans, the great mass of humanity are *not* people toward whom one has no obligations and responsibilities and who likewise feel none toward them; they are, rather, merely people toward whom one does not have immediate or specific obligations. They are people one identifies with in general if not in particular. For the French, however, they are people one does not identify with at all. "No matter where they're from," Polly Platt writes,

> no matter how powerful or underprivileged, whether strangers or acquaintances, Americans deal with each other and everyone else in the world in a manner known as "friendly."
>
> The French don't…. There isn't even a word in the language meaning "friendly" with its resonance of spontaneous warmth toward everybody. *Amical*, the closest French word to "friendly," can only be defined in terms of what the person referred to is not: if a person is *amical*, all it means is that they're not hostile. (1995, 24)

The next dialogue, "Dinner on Friday," explores much the same territory, though it deals in this case not with how one interacts with strangers but with acquaintances.

The key remark in this dialogue is M. Javert's reference to Mr. Johnson as his *"new* colleague." These two men haven't known each other very long (their wives have never even met), which means the Johnsons are outsiders—it would take more than a business relationship to make them anything else—and as such they will be kept at the usual polite remove. They are not going to be dining at the Javerts' home, in other words, not going to be allowed access to their private world (which is for their ingroup), as Mr. Johnson mistakenly assumes when he says, "Let us know if we can bring anything." They will, rather, be dining at a restaurant where the French typically entertain all but their closest intimates—and where you don't need to bring anything.

The Johnsons will no doubt be taken aback, perhaps even offended, when they find out they aren't going to M. Javert's home, for it will seem to them the Javerts are reserved, even unfriendly. What kind of people don't invite an office colleague to their home for dinner? The French, actually, and most other Europeans for that matter. The Johnsons *shouldn't* be thinking like this, of course, applying their American cultural conditioning to French behavior, but they don't know enough about the French to apply any other standard. If they did know more, however, they would realize the Javerts were only trying to make them (the Johnsons) feel comfortable, being careful not to embarrass them by inviting them to their home, thereby suggesting what is certainly not the case, that they were intimates.

Even when someone *is* invited into a French person's home, a sign of very high regard, one's access may be limited. In her book *Cultural Misunderstandings: The French-American Experience*, Carroll tells the story of a "French informant [who] told me that he had never entered the kitchen at his grandmother's house, where he ate lunch once a week, until she became very old and less mobile and resigned herself to sending him to get things from the kitchen during meals" (1988, 15).

Of the three Americans in these dialogues, Patricia (in "Meeting Jeanette") is in for the biggest shock. She and her French friend Monique are out walking and have just run into Monique's friend Jeanette, whom Patricia naturally assumes she is about to meet. ("Take your time. I enjoy meeting your friends.") But Patricia is mistaken; Monique will not in fact be introducing her to Jeanette, because Monique doesn't want to be rude. This will be a stretch for Patricia, who thinks *not* introducing Jeanette is the rude part, but it makes perfect sense in Monique's world. While in America a friend of a friend is practically your own friend, in France friendship is much more of an ex-clusive club; a friend of a friend, especially if these two have never met before, is nothing more than a stranger. And as we have noted above, strangers in France are care-ful not to intrude upon each other. Hence, Monique natu-rally assumes that Jeannette and Patricia, two perfect strangers, fully expect to be left alone, and she is certainly not about to impose them upon each other. If either of them takes the initiative to reach out on her own, that's fine, but it's not Monique's place to tear down the wall between strangers.

"I've clocked introductions by Americans in public places," Platt writes.

> It's almost instantaneous, [after] about five seconds. [But] you can wait until the cows come home in France. This isn't rudeness; it's another marvel of

politeness à la Française. For [the French], it's in-
discreet to introduce people at an accidental encounter. One of them might not wish to be known
to the other. (1995, 245)

Why do the French draw such a tight circle around
themselves? Why do they go to such lengths to protect
their privacy? In part, this is a lesson learned from their
past which, as Stuart Miller points out, has not always featured human nature at its best and has, accordingly, taught
the French (and most Europeans) to be wary. European
history, Miller writes, is a "tale of a world painful and un-
safe" (1990, 5). For the last 2500 years,

one year in five is a year of armed conflict [and]
war is a normal condition....
     Only by plunging ourselves into a sense of the
enormous weight of historic violence can we begin to understand the European soul. We must
think of a vast South Bronx of a continent, repeatedly devastated not for ten or twenty years but, as
men experience time, forever....
     The background of collective violence, com-
bined with other historical forces like memories of
massive poverty, makes the European closed and
defended in ways that are typically un-American.
(17)

Another factor influencing personal interactions is the
deep social stratification that has been a part of French
culture for centuries. While class distinctions and social
standing count for less than they once did (though they
still count for more in France than elsewhere in northern
Europe), they imbue French interpersonal relations with

more formality and ritual politeness than most Americans
are either used to or comfortable with. French people tend
to know the social class of other French people, and while
this is not always a dominant influence in social interactions, it is definitely part of the mix.

Population density (as noted in the previous chapter)
is much higher in Europe than it is in the United States,
while the proportion of people who live in their own homes
is considerably lower; 75 percent of Americans live in
single-family homes, for example, versus only 32 percent
of the French (Zeldin 1996, 175). Since they cannot be
separated by space, the French have to separate themselves
by their behavior. What might be called the immobility
factor, the fact that many French people fully expect to
live out their lives in or very near the same village or neighborhood they grew up in, also serves as a brake on rushing
into relationships.

What about Americans' instincts in dealing with other
people? As with the French, history plays a major role. If
Americans are not threatened by people they don't know,
if strangers don't automatically equate with danger, it is in
part because war and violence do not loom as large in the
American national experience (though it must be noted
that it looms exceedingly large in the national experience
of Native Americans who, incidentally, do not share many
of the European-American attitudes toward strangers, toward people outside their clan or tribal group). The United
States has never been invaded (if you discount the brief
British incursions during the War of 1812) nor has it known
much war on its own soil (except, again, for the Civil War
and the Indian Wars). Their historical conditioning has
not taught Americans the need to protect themselves from
others but rather the need to reach out and connect with

them. In the early days, and later, out on the frontier, circumstances forced people to seek out and befriend strangers. Even if they had reason to distrust other people, they
simply could not afford to avoid each other. No less a person than George Washington was said to have employed a
retainer to linger at the crossroads nearest to Mt. Vernon
"to invite any casual passerby to enliven the dinner table
with news of the outside world" (Boorstin 1958, 305).
Washington's motive was no doubt the desire for news,
not to meet new people; all the same there is certainly no
sense here that one had to be worried about whom one
invited into one's home.

The American attitude toward people one doesn't
know is also influenced by that deep egalitarian strain
mentioned earlier (Dialogue 18, "Knowing Your Stuff,"
page 101). In a society where everyone is equal, it's not
possible to make the mistake of approaching someone
above or beneath your station. You might offend someone's
personal sensibilities by engaging them in conversation, a
shy or reserved person, for example, but you wouldn't be
making a *cultural* mistake. For many centuries the European experience was quite different: distinctions of class
and rank were finely drawn and scrupulously observed, and
people developed elaborate formulas about who they could
approach, how they should approach them, who spoke first,
who could look whom in the eye, and what they could
talk about. "Because of the diminished sense of [national-
ity] and class differences among Americans," John McElroy
has noted,

> their manners became simpler and less formal than
> the manners of Europeans. Even in colonial times,
> it appears, Americans had that inquisitive friend-

liness that still causes them to initiate conversations with strangers, and to ask rather personal questions on short-acquaintance—a behavior that is uncommon in European culture. (1999, 210)

Clearly, then, when it comes to personal relations, the French and the Americans have very different instincts. The upshot is that Americans often come across as forward, intrusive, and overbearing. They sometimes embarrass the French by their openness, at how quickly they reveal things about themselves, and by insisting on intimacy, on receiving it as well as offering it, long before the French deem it appropriate. In the end they often drive the French to be even more reserved and distant than they are already perceived to be by the typical American. Americans should give their French acquaintances more time to open up; they should wait for intimacies to be initiated rather than initiating them; and they should be careful not to interpret French reserve as lack of warmth.

The French, meanwhile, strike many Americans as distant, guarded, and even cold. Americans tend to interpret the French instinct to grant other people their privacy as aloofness and may even put it down as just another manifestation of French arrogance and rudeness. In dealing with Americans, the French should not mistake American openness for prying or friendliness for aggressiveness, and they should not be afraid of compromising their privacy if they open up more than they would with other French.

3

Americans and the Germans

Dialogues 35–51

Germans and Americans are surprisingly tolerant and forgiving of each other; they seem to excuse each other's lapses
and accept each other's excuses quite readily, which is not
quite as true for Americans and the French or Americans
and the British. Germans still tend to look down on Americans, but where the French tend to regard Americans with
disdain and the British, with condescension, the Germans
look on Americans more with disappointment. For their
part, Americans tend to see more of themselves in the Germans than they do in the other two cultures and to feel a
closer affinity with German cultural norms and values. There
are important cultural differences, of course, enough to fill up
the rest of this chapter, but the similarities are noteworthy.

German culture seems to have far fewer trappings of an aristocratic past than either England or France. This makes Germany much more like a meritocracy—where people are "self-made," where they succeed and are judged by their accomplishments rather than their social class—of the kind that has evolved in the United States. German and American workplace norms are also quite similar, in part for this same reason, and Germans and Americans both tend to be direct in their speech. Indeed, Germans are one of the handful of nationalities Americans find to be direct. Like Americans, Germans tend to be quite sensitive to criticism and to care what other countries think of them (which is generally much less true of the English and not at all the case with the French).

As for why the two cultures are alike, John Ardagh points out that if you

> exclude the Welsh, Scots, and Irish, more Americans are of German than English origin. Small surprise that so many prominent Americans have German names. Maybe this also helps to explain why the two peoples are in some ways so similar: they may differ greatly in their degree of social formality, but they share something of the same business ethos, the same liking for thoroughness, efficiency and modernism and the same fondness for litigation. (1995, 569)

Nearly fifty-five million Americans, more than one-sixth of the total population, claim at least partial German heritage.

None of this is to say that Americans and Germans can let down their cultural guard when doing business together, but it does mean that there may be more intuitive understanding between these two peoples than in the case of the other two cultural pairings in this book.

Dialogues

35. Shortcut

LINDA: Let's cut across this field.

MAX: Using this road, you mean?

LINDA: Right.

MAX: It's probably a private road.

LINDA: But there's no sign.

MAX: Precisely.

36. Moving to Anhalt

MARY: So. It's official. The plant will close next fall.

HANS: Yes, after so many years. I started here twenty years ago. My father got me a job with him, in the motor pool. It will be hard to start all over.

MARY: Well at least there's good news.

The plant they're opening up in
Anhalt will be needing experienced people like you.

HANS: No doubt. I've never been to
Anhalt, but I hope to visit one
day. I wonder what it's like.

MARY: You'll find out soon enough, I
guess.

HANS: How do you mean?

37. Weekend Workers

BOB: We got a bit behind on this. The
deadline is Wednesday.

HORST: Yes. We'll have to clear our
calendar and work on it first
thing next week.

BOB: That'll be cutting it a bit close,
don't you think?

HORST: What other choice do we have?

BOB: We could come in on Saturday.

38. Dirty Sink

HELEN: Did you read the ad copy?

FRITZ: I liked most of it, except for the
part that said "This will never
stain your sink."

HELEN: What's wrong with that?

FRITZ: We should say, "If used properly,
it will never stain your sink."

HELEN: Of course, but people know that.

FRITZ: Probably, but we want them to be encouraged by our ad.

HELEN: Of course, that's why we have to come on strong.

39. Quality

ROGER: Brauner is battering us again, with their new offer.

GUDRUN: Yes, their price is hard to beat.

ROGER: We'll have to cut our costs some-how.

GUDRUN: Why?

ROGER: To get our price down.

GUDRUN: That could affect quality.

ROGER: Of course, but we've got to stay competitive.

GUDRUN: My point exactly.

40. Love Life

ANN: What's wrong with Klaus?

BIRGIT: He broke up with his girlfriend.

ANN: Poor guy. He looks so unhappy.

BIRGIT: He's taking it very hard.

ANN So what can we do to help?

BIRGIT: Help?

41. Feedback

CATHY: Who do you think she'll pick to chair that task force?

IRMGARD: I think you have a good chance.

CATHY: Me? No way. She doesn't think much of me.

IRMGARD: I don't agree. Why do you say that?

CATHY: She's never said anything to me about my work.

IRMGARD: Then why are you so worried?

42. Surprise

MICHAEL: Marketing is going to get a new manager.

HEIDI: It's about time. That department's not as efficient as it used to be. Who do you think they'll give the job to?

MICHAEL: I think Schmidt will get it. He's a real original, and he's not afraid to bend the rules. He'll shake things up a bit.

HEIDI: He certainly has a fertile mind. He's also quite unpredictable.

MICHAEL: Exactly. Someone who will surprise us.

43. Thinking on Your Feet

HELGA: Did you finish the training design?

ALICE: Not quite.

HELGA: I'll call Bosch then.

ALICE: What for?

HELGA: To reschedule the presentation.

ALICE: After all we went through to get this meeting? We can improvise if it comes to that.

HELGA: Improvise?

ALICE: You know, think on our feet.

44. Rude

TODD: Dieter is so rude.

ELKE: What happened?

TODD: He said my office was a mess.

ELKE: But it is.

TODD: And he said it makes us look bad when people visit.

ELKE: So why do you say he's rude?

45. Closing Costs

PAUL: The yearly figures are in. Freiburg's last again.

HANNAH: Too bad. The plant's really too small to be efficient anymore. It's

lasted a long time, though, more
than fifty years.

PAUL: We should probably close it. We
can find jobs for those people
easily.

HANNAH: That's what two of the multinationals did, moved out three years
ago. We're the only manufacturing plant left there now.

PAUL: Yes, we probably should have
acted faster.

46. Team Leader

PAMELA: Who are you going to pick to lead
the negotiations?

GERHARD: I was thinking about Dr. Mueller.

PAMELA: He's very serious, isn't he?

GERHARD: Quite. He thinks deeply about
things.

PAMELA: He's not one to make jokes,
either.

GERHARD: So you favor him too?

47. Misleading

HELMUT: Did Schmidt show you his report?

FRANK: Yes. It needs a lot of work.

HELMUT: Did you tell him?

FRANK: I told him it was a good start.

HELMUT: You shouldn't have misled him.

FRANK: What do you mean?

48. Slow Going

CAROL: We've got a week to get this design to manufacturing.

BRIGID: Engineering hasn't finished its review yet. They're very thorough, as you know.

CAROL: The new Feuer product will be in stores in six weeks.

BRIGID: They must have started before we did. Or else they've got more people working on it.

CAROL: Our engineering review process is just too long.

BRIGID: Our engineers don't miss much, that's for sure.

CAROL: Except their deadlines. I'm going to ask Herr Neuger if he can come up with any shortcuts in the process.

49. A Hunch

RALPH: Something tells me we should try this approach.

GRETA: Something you read?

RALPH: No. It's just a hunch I've got.

GRETA: A feeling, you mean?

RALPH: Right. I can't really explain it, but I'm usually right about these things.

50. Hello Christian

FRANZ: Dr. Wilson. Good to see you again.

DAVID: Hey, Franz. How are you?

FRANZ: Fine, thank you. I want you to meet a colleague of mine. Dr. Christian Kuntsler, may I present Dr. David Wilson.

DAVID: Christian. A pleasure to meet you.

CHRISTIAN: My pleasure entirely, Dr. Wilson.

51. Lunch at the Rathskeller

TED: Where shall we go for lunch?

OTTO: Let's try Die Rathskeller.

TED: Why don't we ask Hans to join us?

OTTO: Who's that?

TED: You know. The new guy who started in Karl's division yesterday.

OTTO: I haven't met him yet.
TED: Now's your chance.

Analyses, Dialogues 35–51

35. Shortcut

We begin our look at the Germans with what is perhaps their most important cultural characteristic: a passion for order. The Germans are greatly comforted by order and orderliness, and especially by what it promises: security, predictability, and stability. They are, as a consequence, equally fond of anything that contributes to or helps maintain order, such as discipline, conformity, precedents, plans, rules, regulations, policies, and procedures. "In Germany, one breathes in love of order with the air," Jerome K. Jerome wrote, "[and] the babies beat time with their rattles" (in Yapp 1988, 194). In a 1989 survey, Europeans were asked what it was about their nationality that made them most proud; for Germans the most common source of pride was *Grundgesetz,* or basic law (Mole 1995, 29). The German love of order, incidentally, is not hard to explain: order is the antidote to angst, to unease or insecurity—and angst is the German national disease.

The Germans have a "devotion to order," Richard Hill has observed.

Lenin is reputed to have said that the Germans
always buy platform tickets before they storm a rail-
way station. Whether he was right or not, an everyday reality of daily life [in Germany] is rules that
forbid mowing a lawn on Sundays or between the
hours of 1 and 3 P.M., putting glass in a dustbin after 8 P.M., taking a shower in your own flat after 10
P.M. and, in the case of the good city of Hamm,
allowing your dog to bark between 7 P.M. and 8 A.M.
(1994, 34)

The Germans hate gray areas and like to go by the
book. And if something isn't in the book, Germans panic.
Not surprisingly, they score very high on what Geert
Hofstede calls the "uncertainty avoidance" scale. In his
famous study of IBM in more than forty countries, Hofstede
measured how people in various cultures cope with the
uncertainty that is inherent in life. "Extreme uncertainty,"
he notes, "creates intolerable anxiety, and human society
has developed ways to cope with the inherent uncertainty
of our living on the brink of an [unknown] future" (1988,
111). Hofstede found that while some cultures live easily
with uncertainty—rolling with life's punches, as it were—
others fear and are threatened by it. The latter cultures,
accordingly, go to great lengths either to eliminate uncertainty altogether, where that is possible, or, where it is not,
to minimize its impact and control its consequences. Anything that can be done to predict the future, for example,
or protect oneself from the unknown has great appeal in
such cultures. Uncertainty can't be eliminated entirely, of
course, but life can be arranged so as to cushion the blows.

Their love of certainty and the lengths they will go to
secure it are the source of one of the most common com-
plaints made about the Germans (often by themselves):

that they are too rigid. As Germans see it, if being inflexible and unyielding can buy them security in an unstable world, the price may just be worth it. Or, as one veteran German watcher put it, "Germans often view giving up certain individual rights as a fair trade in creating a better and more ordered society" (Nees 2000, 49). So it is that whenever Germans are in doubt or come across an ambiguous situation—two circumstances the Germans loathe—their instinct is to regulate, preferring to err on the side of prohibiting behavior rather than allowing it.

For their part, Americans have almost the opposite instinct. Where Germans are willing to give up freedom if it will buy security, Americans are much more likely to sacrifice security if it will buy freedom. They have never been particularly daunted by the unknown or the unexpected; they like to know what can be known, of course (they don't cultivate surprise for its own sake), but they're not afraid of or threatened by uncertainty. They're not easily thrown by the unexpected and are in fact famous for their ability to cope with change. American companies are renowned for the ease with which they reinvent themselves, often from the ground up, something that generally takes longer and causes more pain in Europe (if it is even attempted). Not surprisingly, on Hofstede's uncertainty index, which measures how comfortable people in different countries are with the uncertainty inherent in life, Germans (at 65) are 19 points higher (more anxious about uncertainty) than Americans (at 46) are. (The range is from 112, most anxious, to 8, least anxious.)

Americans are also temperamentally disinclined toward rules, order, and security, and they certainly don't value them *for their own sake* as the Germans seem to. These regulations all seem a bit limiting to them, and if there's anything highly individualistic, freedom-loving Americans hate, it's limits. They would rather not regulate, therefore, unless they are forced to, much preferring to keep their options open and allow themselves as much flexibility and room to maneuver as possible. Their assumption, accordingly, is that if something is not expressly prohibited, then it must be allowed.

All of which brings us to Max and Linda and this short-cut across a field. Linda sees no sign on the road and assumes, therefore, that it must be okay to use it. Max, who assumes something is prohibited unless it is expressly permitted, interprets the absence of a sign to mean just the opposite.

The Germans come by their love of order and desire for control honestly enough, mainly as the legacy of an especially unsettled past. "For centuries," Greg Nees points out, "Germany has been a major battlefield for both civil and European wars, and this has left a deep mark on the German psyche. These wars brought with them chaos and suffering and destroyed the social and economic advances Germans had worked so hard to achieve" (2000, 41). Nees notes that the German devotion to order may also be motivated by a desire to temper their opposite, irrational instinct—"the wild and romantic side of their German personality"—which, when unchecked, leads to "havoc and turmoil" that frighten and embarrass Germans (41–42).

The American experience has been all about embracing and dealing with the unknown. America was the New World, after all, uncertainty incarnate; people who couldn't handle the unknown didn't get into tiny boats and sail across the North Atlantic to alien shores. The early immigrants to America were almost immediately out of their depth, faced with a bewildering variety of unprecedented circumstances and unfamiliar situations for which life in the Old World had done almost nothing to prepare them. Indeed, one of the first things Americans had to learn to do, if they wanted to survive, was to discard years of habit, tradition, and precedent and place their trust in the untried and the untested. They were making it up as they went along and could ill afford to get hung up on rules or indulge in any other kind of inflexibility.

In their dealings with each other, Germans and Americans bump up against this key cultural difference regularly, and it usually serves to confirm and reinforce deep-seated concerns each side has about the other. Germans are frequently appalled at American indifference to order and stability, at their desire to leave things as open, undefined, and unregulated as possible so as not to be "tied down," and at the ease with which Americans embrace change, their much-vaunted ability to "turn on a dime." It's also alarming to Germans how willing Americans are to circumvent or even change the rules in the name of efficiency and getting things done. This sometimes has a short-term payoff, as even Germans recognize, but the long-term effect on the social order is rarely worth the price. So it is that Americans come across as reckless, short-sighted, and undisciplined, which makes Germans wary, suspicious, and reluctant to trust them.

Americans, on the other hand, are constantly brought up short by what they experience as German inflexibility and rigidity. Germans are hung up on rules and regulations, on the right way to do things, and obsessed with order and stability. They are afraid of anything new or different and extremely reluctant—and very slow—to change, requiring endless assurances (studies, data, trials, testimonials) before taking even the slightest risk. They strike Americans as uptight, timid, and excessively cautious.

In their interactions with Germans, Americans need to prepare the ground much more thoroughly for new initiatives or changes in policies or regulations and also give Germans longer to come around. For their part, Germans will have more luck dealing with Americans if they show a greater willingness to compromise and take the occasional risk.

36. Moving to Anhalt

On the whole Germans are much less mobile than Americans are. Generation after generation grow up in the same village or region (*Heimat*), and you naturally identify strongly with the place you—and most everyone you know—come from. The general lack of mobility also guarantees that you grow up surrounded by an extended family and an unchanging circle of family friends and acquaintances, with whom, naturally, you also come to identify. Under these circumstances moving amounts to much more than physically changing places; it means cutting your identity loose from its moorings and going off to live among strangers, among people you may never come to know and by whom you may never be truly known. "Germans are intensely loyal to their Heimat," Greg Nees writes,

> the local area where they were born and raised.
> Unlike Americans, who are known for their willingness to pick up and move when an economic opportunity presents itself, Germans have traditionally been far less willing to leave their local region.... Because of the stigma attached to Germany's past, many citizens tend to place more importance on their regional rather than their na-

tional identity. One person from the south of Germany (Bavarians are especially well known for their regional loyalty) declared, "I am Bavarian first, European second, and German third." (2000, 27)

Needless to say, the generous benefits Germany offers its unemployed citizens is another, more practical reason why Germans stay put, as is the fact that German companies take their responsibilities for their workers seriously and try to make generous provisions for them in the event of plant closings (see Dialogue 45, "Closing Costs," pages 189–90).

For Americans, as noted above, mobility is practically a way of life and in a sense almost a cultural imperative; if one believes in success, then one had better be willing to move. More than forty million Americans, one-sixth of the population, change their address every year, 38 percent live outside the state where they were born, and approximately half the residents of the major American cities change every decade (McElroy 1999, 87). "Many visitors were impressed with how readily Americans moved from one place to another," Richard Pells has written,

> how prevalent their assumption that they could improve their luck by changing their address or embarking on a new career. To Europeans who normally went to school, married, and spent their adult years living in the same house and working at the same job, all within a few miles from where they were born, America appeared to be a nation of nomads.... Once past adolescence, children invariably left home, relocating in another part of the country. To stay put was a sign of failure. (1997, 170)

In the dialogue, Hans and Mary completely misunderstand each other because of their different notions of mobility. Hans mentions to Mary how difficult it will be "to start all over" now that the plant in his town is closing down, assuming that she understands he is talking about starting over in a new job in that same town, his Heimat. But if Mary assumes anything, it would be that Hans will move to Anhalt where they will "be needing experienced people" like him. Hans, wondering what Mary's reply has to do with his predicament, and especially what is so good about the news of the plant opening in Anhalt, now signals once again that he's not moving when he says he's "never been to Anhalt" but hopes to visit one day. But for an American like Mary, never having been to a place where job opportunities are opening up would hardly constitute a reason for an unemployed person not to move there. Hence her answer ("You'll find out soon enough, I guess"), which is yet another non sequitur for Hans.

What makes the Germans such a rooted race? For one thing, moving is fraught with risk and uncertainty, and we saw in the first dialogue how little the Germans enjoy that. Moreover, as we have observed elsewhere, Europeans in general live in a world of finite possibilities, where it is safe to think small and be thankful for what one has been given. If this is your outlook on life, that it offers only limited opportunities, then surely one place is just as good as another. In all probability, the grass is *not* in fact greener on the other side of the fence, and even if it is, the sacrifices it would take to get there are daunting. As Stuart Miller has noted, the evidence of history, "a past in which, for more than two thousand years, social and economic movement were utterly exceptional," prevents the average European "from seeing himself or others as 'going anywhere'" (1990, 54).

Needless to say, taking chances (such as moving)

doesn't really fit into this picture. A chance, after all, in-volves risk; risk can result in failure; and failure, in a world of limited opportunities, is a deeply sobering prospect. This idea of limited possibilities may be changing, however, with the advent of the European Union. When your range as a worker was effectively confined to your own country, op-portunities may have seemed limited, but if your range is suddenly widened to all of Europe, there may indeed be greener pastures out there.

As for Americans, moving is practically in the national genes. The immigrants who founded America were deter-mined to make a better life for themselves (those who came willingly, that is), and they believed deeply in the possi-bility of continuous self-improvement. They were willing to cross an ocean for this belief, and, in a sense, they never stopped moving, for no matter how well they did in one location (or perhaps *because* they did so well), there seemed to be no reason they could not do even better elsewhere. While they may have been restless and discontent before they came, with all avenues to a better life blocked, they were even more restless after they arrived—and found few limits whatsoever to realizing their dreams. If they took things too far in their exuberance, to the point of never being satisfied no matter how much they achieved, they can perhaps be excused. It should be noted that the use of the same language all across the continent greatly abetted the nomadic instincts of Americans. "Americans," Howard Jones has written,

> have not only had, or thought we had, plenty of
> natural resources, we have had, or thought we had,
> plenty of space into which to run. The effects of
> this grand and simple assumption upon American

development have been enormous. The American
family is more often rootless than not because the
younger generation could—and can—always go
somewhere else.... [While] it was impossible in
France or Germany for a local Horace Greeley to
advise the young, "Go West, young man, go west,"
this was natural, indeed inevitable in the United
States. (1968, 386–87)

37. Weekend Workers

A story is told about the German branch of an American
multinational pharmaceutical company preparing for the
launch of a new product on the German market. The
American executive in charge set the launch date for a
Saturday and invited all employees and their families to
the kickoff, which was to include an elaborate picnic. The
Germans, however, were quite upset about having to come
in on their weekend, and in the end the launch had to be
rescheduled, at considerable inconvenience and expense.

   Germans, like most Europeans (and including the
French and British—see Dialogue 3, " A New Director,"
page 24 and Dialogue 20, "Working Late," page 102), insist on drawing a line between the demands of one's job
and employer and the obligations to self and family (and
strong German labor unions make sure this line is respected). They are, accordingly, extremely protective of
their personal life and try to keep it as separate as possible
from their professional life. When they are on the job, they
give it their complete attention and energy, but when they
are away from their job, they expect to be left alone. Although it's not quite a social taboo to ask someone to come

in on the weekend, it would certainly be a last resort. "There is a clear demarcation between private and business life," John Mole observes.

> They leave work as punctually as they arrive and rarely take work home. They do not like being called at home on business unless there is a very good reason. People at all levels take their full holiday entitlement, and they do not keep in touch with the office when they are away or expect to be called. (1995, 39)

Germans are in fact very good at compartmentalizing, and this ability to keep separate the various dimensions of their lives comes quite naturally to them.

None of this is to suggest that Germans are not dedicated workers or that they have no regard for the fortunes of the company. Indeed, German workers are probably more loyal and committed to their employers than are their American counterparts (who, for example, change employers much more frequently). The difference is in the distance Germans like to keep between their private life and the world of work.

In the United States the line between work and one's personal life is not quite so absolute. While managers might hesitate before asking workers to come in on a weekend, it's not unthinkable. Nor would American employees balk at attending a company-sponsored social event on a weekend, so long as it wasn't mandatory. Americans cherish their private lives too, but they are generally less protective of them and more understanding if the world of work occasionally intrudes.

In the dialogue, then, Bob assumes he is proposing the standard remedy for a deadline that's about to be missed: namely, coming in on the weekend. But if he were listening closely, he would hear two strong indications that this is not at all the standard practice in Germany. The first is Horst's rejoinder: "We'll have to clear our calendar and work on it first thing next week." Presumably, Horst is as aware as Bob of the upcoming weekend, so there must be a reason he doesn't allude to it. But even if Bob misses this first clue, the next one is unmistakable: "What other choice do we have?" Clearly, Horst has ruled out the weekend and means what other choice do they have except the beginning of next week. But Bob hasn't ruled out the weekend, of course, and now suggests it, no doubt to Horst's surprise.

Though Bob doesn't realize it, he and Horst were on different tracks from the very beginning, with Bob's first words: "We got a bit behind on this." In those exceedingly rare cases when Germans *could* be persuaded to come in on a weekend, they would certainly not do so if the necessity was the result of poor planning, which is what Bob's comment seems to suggest. It is through planning, after all, that people can control and manipulate the future, something very important to security-loving Germans. Poor planning, therefore, is inexcusable and would never constitute a reason to give up one's weekend.

Another part of the reason Germans hold their weekends so sacrosanct may be because they are not as inclined as Americans to befriend or even socialize with colleagues from work. (Germans also don't like to be business partners with their friends, in marked contrast with the French, who *prefer* to do business with members of their ingroup.) It may be, therefore, that compared with Americans, Germans work harder when they are on the job—because they socialize less—and have more need of their time away from work to relax. And it surely means that a German's time away from work may be the only opportunity he or she has to be with close friends.

Another element here may be the fact that middle- and upper-class Europeans tend to be a more naturally cultured people (see Dialogue 18, "Knowing Your Stuff," page 101), instinctively drawn to the arts and philosophy, for example, or to the pursuit of truth and beauty. These are not peripheral or secondary concerns the way they tend to be in the United States, something one cultivates or indulges in if one has the time. Rather, the development of one's inner life, sometimes called the life of the mind, is part of what makes for a well-rounded person, a fully developed adult, which is a responsibility Europeans take seriously. Needless to say, this kind of personal development takes time, which may be why Germans are so protective of their time away from work (and also helps explain why Europeans have so much more vacation time than Americans do).

Americans have been accused of not having inner lives, and while that is an unkind exaggeration, it is probably true that what passes for a fully developed adult in the United States would not pass for one in Europe. Be that as it may, Americans believe that you can just as easily develop yourself at work as anywhere else—it is experience that makes a person who he or she is, not sophistication and manners—which means that Americans might feel they were sacrificing much less to come in on the weekend than would the average German.

38. Dirty Sink

The truth is something of an obsession with Germans. They have an exceptionally high regard for objectivity and accuracy—is it any wonder they make the world's best measuring devices?—and pride themselves on seeing things exactly as they are, neither better nor worse. This core value manifests itself in all manner of characteristic German attitudes and behaviors: an insistence on being precise, for example; the favoring of reason over emotion (though the Germans can be hopelessly romantic); a passion for fairness; and the importance of honesty and plain speaking (some would say bluntness). When it comes from a German, the truth will always be unvarnished, no matter how harsh or unpleasant it may sound. Indeed, for Germans the truth never seems to "hurt" as it sometimes does in other cultures. Even if it were to hurt on occasion, knowing the truth is well worth the price, for the truth, after all, eliminates uncertainty.

Just as they fearlessly dispense the truth, Germans expect nothing less in return. They have no patience, for example, with the usual dodges, the face-saving tactics other cultures often use to blunt the force of truth, such as half-truths, white lies, sugarcoating, or the proverbial pulling of one's punches. Germans don't need to be protected from the truth; they can handle it. To a German, not telling the truth is not merely lying; it's practically an insult.

Which brings us to exaggeration, the trait on display in the dialogue. Exaggeration, after all, is a way of making fast and loose with the truth, and it deeply offends German sensibilities. They don't trust anyone who exaggerates, who does not see—or at least does not describe—things as they are. Exaggeration also makes Germans very suspicious. Why would people claim more for their product or their company than they were capable of delivering? Does it mean they don't think people will take them seriously otherwise? Or do they think that perhaps people won't know they're exaggerating and will somehow be fooled? "In general," Edward T. and Mildred Reed Hall have observed, "Americans are inclined toward overstatement…, particularly in advertising and promotion, [whereas] Germans avoid it. Germans think Americans blow things out of proportion as if they are afraid they won't receive enough attention unless they indulge in hyperbole" (1990, 51).

For Americans exaggeration is a harmless game, at least in the arena of advertising, where this dialogue is set (and which is practically synonymous with "hype"). To Americans exaggeration is not fooling around with the truth as much as it is looking on the bright side and putting things in the best possible light. Americans, it must be remembered, are firm believers in what they call the power of positive thinking. But to Germans, thinking positively is as nonsensical as thinking negatively. What's important, of course, is to think *clearly*.

Helen is somewhat taken aback, then, when Fritz objects to a little harmless overstatement ("This will never stain your sink"). But Fritz knows that customers want the truth (German customers, that is) and that anything that seems to stray from the truth, that promises more than the customer knows is possible, will be disturbing and ultimately counterproductive. Hence, he wants to say "If used properly, [the product] will never stain your sink," a straightforward claim the company could verify if necessary. Being clear-eyed and objective about the product will reassure the German customer, who will then "be encouraged" by the ad.

But in Helen's world, customers "know that," meaning they know better than to take ads literally. Indeed, they have long since gotten used to advertising that makes extravagant claims, so used to it, in fact, that if the hype is not there, customers miss it and begin to have doubts. Hence Helen's injunction, "We have to come on strong," meaning the ad has to exaggerate to have any chance of being taken seriously. It is interesting, in this context, to note how American advertising has in recent years begun to make increasing use of plain speech and even understatement, wherein it is precisely the absence of overstatement which makes the point. We don't have to exaggerate, these ads seem to say, to get your attention—which is nothing more than the exception which proves the rule.

Why do Americans so often take refuge in hyperbole? Why don't they trust the unadorned truth? Part of the answer is that the United States is a market-driven society, where for many people psychological and material success is directly or indirectly a function of selling somebody something. But it is more than that; Americans are also an exuberant, hopeful, irrepressible people. Their tendency to exaggerate is all of a piece with their innate optimism and their deeply held belief in progress, in the notion that however good things may be, they can always be improved. This sentiment animates the American national character and makes Americans the strivers and achievers they are. It means, among other things, that Americans are never satisfied with the status quo; even before a new product has reached the market, the people back in R&D are already working on the next generation, the new and improved version. In a world where anything is possible— just give us a little more time—and things always seem to get better, one exaggerates almost as a matter of course; today's exaggeration, after all, is almost guaranteed to be tomorrow's reality. Daniel Boorstin has observed that

> Statements which foreigners took for lies or brag-
> gadocio, American speakers intended to be vaguely

clairvoyant. The American booster often was simply speaking in the future tense, asserting what could not yet be disproved. Even in colonial times men writing about America had found it hard to confine themselves to demonstrable facts.

[Later], especially in the booming West, men acquired a habit of innocent overstatement. They seldom said less than they intended.... "City" replaced "town," "university" designated an institution which in Europe might have been called a "college," and "college" became a name for almost any educational effort, however meager its resources. Even grander words described institutions that hardly existed at all. The elegant "hotel" was widely applied to ramshackle, flea-bitten inns and taverns. Americans thought they were not exaggerating but only anticipating—describing things which had not quite yet "gone through the formality of actually taking place." (1965, 296, 297)

Indeed, for true believers like Americans, *not* to exaggerate, not to make somewhat inflated claims for one's product or capabilities, feels almost defeatist. While the Germans pride themselves on being realists, to Americans, realists are just people without any vision.

39. Quality

Germans insist on quality, both as producers and consumers of goods, and when it comes to quality, German products easily hold their own against the world's best. High quality comes at a price, quite literally, and usually a rather steep one, but the German view is that people will pay more if they are convinced they're getting more. For Germans, in other words, it is quality and not price that ultimately makes a product competitive. "Activities [in Germany] are product-led," David Hickson and Derek Pugh have observed,

> with an emphasis on competition through product appropriateness and quality, rather than market-led, with an emphasis on competition through price. This can lead to over-engineering when only products which are "better" but more expensive are offered to the market. The impact of marketing has usually been limited to advertising and selling the good product or service (including after-sales service) for the long-term, rather than in determining how to satisfy the consumer's immediate needs at a lower price. (1995, 98)

For Germans the only proper role that price should play is to reflect quality. Hence, prices aren't usually lowered merely to sell a product, for that means the price wasn't fair to begin with. And fairness in pricing is an article of faith with German consumers. "To the Germans," Robert Moran has written,

> it is a sign of bad business or bad preparation when discussion over price leads the seller to drop the price several times in an attempt to gain the sale at any cost. Generally the Germans are more structural and rigid in their dealings. They feel they have developed a quality product and have set a fair price for it. (1992, 38)

Americans want quality too, but they're not fixated on it. It's a very important factor in the mix, of course, a big part of what makes a product or service attractive, but it must be weighed against the other factors that keep businesses in business, such as time-to-market, inventory, costs, and especially price. In the dialogue Roger clearly regards price as the primary path to competitiveness, which is why his first instinct to meet the challenge from Brauner is to look for a way to reduce costs (hence, price). But this puzzles Gudrun, who puts her faith in quality and is naturally quite alarmed at any move that might threaten it, such as Roger's instinct to tinker with costs. Ultimately, both speakers believe in being competitive; they would just get there by very different routes.

Their high regard for quality is of a piece with the German passion for perfection, for doing the best job you can *on principle* (whether or not that makes you competitive or is better for the customer, though of course it will be). The insistence on quality and perfection, in turn, is no doubt related to the German fear of uncertainty. Simply put, if you make the best car you can, then you eliminate as far as humanly possible any unexpected events. There is no doubt in the German mind that people will select quality, regardless of price, because there is no doubt that people want to minimize risk, failure, and uncertainty. Given time, and this is an important given, quality will always win out over price.

And it turns out the Germans have time, considerably more than their American business counterparts. The main reason is the source of investment capital, which in the United States comes mainly from private stockholders, who are eager to see a quick return on their investment, but which in Germany is more likely to come from central banks, who can afford to wait for their rewards. "A German company," Hickson and Pugh have noted,

will be bank-financed to a much greater degree than
being financed by the stock market—and German
banks take a long-term view. So the emphasis on a
yearly profit and its effects on the share price, and
thus on the market value of the company, is much
less than in, for example, the Anglo economies.
(1995, 98)

It must be remembered in this context that quality takes
longer to reveal itself, at least as compared with price,
which is (or is not) competitive the moment it's an-
nounced. Products and services have to stand the test of
time, to be used by a number of people in a wide variety of
circumstances, thereby developing a history and a reputation. The ability of German companies to take the long
view makes it much easier for Germans to put their faith
in quality, though they would probably do so anyway.

The American attitude toward quality is rooted in part
in a deep and abiding faith in progress. They tend to believe (because their experience has shown them) that however perfect a product we may have today, it's bound to be
eclipsed tomorrow by an even better one. If that's really
the case, if quality is relative, then there comes a time
when price (or color or availability) naturally begins to
compete with it. When that time comes, Americans, unlike Germans, are much more willing to compromise.

Stuart Miller discerns still other currents in the differing American and German attitudes toward quality.

Americans have been more interested in producing something expediently than in producing it ex-
quisitely. The roots of this difference are historically complex. The European aristocracy monopo-
lized nearly all manufactured products and set

higher and higher standards for them.... Though quality has declined, the demand for it still hangs in the air and conditions European attitudes toward products.

American democratic tradition worked the other way. A mass of potential consumers, with little wealth but a normal human attraction to the showy and the luxurious, created a market for goods manufactured quickly, cheaply, and in great numbers and, naturally, of a quality inferior to the aristocratically grounded crafts of Europe. (1990, 179, 180)

Finally, part of Roger's sense of urgency, and Gudrun's lack thereof, may be a function of the age of their respective cultures. Older cultures typically have a deeper appreciation of the sweep of history and of how insignificant one or two generations is in the scheme of things. There is, accordingly, a sense of continuation, that things do not end here, which makes the present and the immediate future a mere blip on the screen. Younger cultures feel pressured by time; their experience has been that there is not very much of it and a great deal to be accomplished. Tomorrow, to say nothing of next week or next month, might be too late. For the Germans next month or next year is just around the corner. American companies put out quarterly financial reports and annual budgets. "German businesses plan for the future," Edward T. Hall and Mildred Reed Hall have written,

> methodically building a solid foundation. They are not preoccupied with immediate results.... and so they find it inconvenient and disruptive to be asked to provide quarterly financial statements and reports; instead they provide annual financial reports.

In some German industries five years is not considered long term and many companies routinely
plan ten and twenty years ahead. (1990, 37)

40. Love Life

This dialogue is about unhappiness—and what can be *done*
about it. For Ann it's pretty simple: a guy named Klaus is
unhappy; people aren't supposed to be unhappy; we have
to "help" him (i.e., make him happy again). But Birgit's
not so sure. Oh, Klaus is unhappy all right, but that's hardly
a call to action. There's nothing broken here, in Birgit's
view, so there's nothing to fix. And there, in a nutshell, is
the Old World and the New at their most opposite.

We should probably start with Ann's assumption that
people aren't supposed to be unhappy. Where does such a
belief come from? It has to do with the notion of locus of
control (see Dialogue 7, "All the Stops," page 26 and Dialogue 31, "Sales Figures," page 108), the concept which
deals with the question of who is ultimately responsible
for what happens in life. In some cultures, and the United
States is probably the preeminent example, the answer is
that what happens in life is ultimately up to the individual.
Not in the sense that the individual is the *cause* of everything that happens, but in the sense that no matter what
happens, regardless of what life dishes up, the individual
can still get the upper hand. This is in many ways the quin-
tessential American belief, the idea that one shapes and is
ultimately responsible for one's own destiny. Indeed, it is
the impulse which created the country in the first place.
Whatever else one may say of the first settlers, they certainly believed in themselves.

Not surprisingly, this outlook on life affects how people view happiness. If you assume that people naturally want to be happy, and if you assume further that people are in control of their lives and can therefore have what they want, then you would expect people in such a world to be happy as a matter of course. Happiness, in other words, would be normal and customary. Needless to say, in such a scheme, unhappiness must necessarily be abnormal. It could only happen, after all, in the unlikely and unfortunate event that a person had somehow lost the ability to control his or her life. And in Ann's world, such a person would clearly need "help."

But not in Birgit's world, where the locus of control is decidedly more external, where people believe that certain things in life are beyond their ability to influence or change—or help. While Germans assume they have some control over what happens to them, they also recognize certain limits, that there are some givens in life that must be accepted. It is what the Spanish poet and philosopher Miguel de Unamuno called "the tragic sense of life," not tragic in the sense of sad or calamitous but more in the sense of inevitable and uncontrollable. According to this worldview, you certainly have a hand in shaping your destiny, but whole parts of it are also shaped for you.

Needless to say, when you're not entirely in control of what happens in life, when you're not writing the script, then neither are you quite so responsible for the outcome, for your happiness or unhappiness. Nor can it be said that one is somehow more natural than the other; by definition both are natural and inevitable. When a person is unhappy, there's really nothing wrong or broken, no more so than when someone is happy. And while you would certainly feel bad for a friend's misfortune, you would not

necessarily feel that something had to—or *could*—be done
about it. What can be done, after all, about the vicissi-
tudes of life? It is interesting in this context to note the
difference in how American and German fairy tales end.
The last line of American fairy tales is an optimistic, if
rather improbable, "They lived happily every after." The
last line in the stories Germans tell their children is a much
more modest and realistic "If they haven't died, they are
still living."

None of this, meanwhile, should be taken to mean that
Germans are inclined to wallow in unhappiness or don't
like to enjoy themselves, but it does mean that with Germans, unlike Americans, there is much more acceptance
of the suffering inherent in the human condition and a
corresponding expectation that life will not always be pleas-
ing. As James Baldwin so famously observed, Europeans,
unlike Americans, have a sense of tragedy.

41. Feedback

Compliments don't flow freely in the German workplace.
Germans seem to believe you should compliment other
people only when they exceed reasonable expectations,
not merely when they meet them. And since the Germans
set expectations very high to begin with, employees rarely
exceed them. Where people are expected to do their best
as a matter of course, as a kind of minimum standard, it is
neither exceptional nor noteworthy—and certainly not
deserving of a compliment—merely to do a good job. *Everybody* does a good job—or should.

Compared with Germans, Americans are quite liberal,
even indiscriminate, with their praise (a charge, in fact,
that Germans often level against them). While Germans

reserve compliments for exceptional achievements, Americans lavish them on the most ordinary of accomplishments. It's not necessary, for example, for a worker to exceed or even meet expectations to be given a word of encouragement. Americans will compliment each other merely for making a good effort, whatever the result, or in some cases just for having a positive attitude. The role of compliments and praise in America is not so much to recognize distinctive achievement as it is to provide reassurance and build confidence. To put it another way, Americans appear to need compliments and encouragement in a way Germans do not. A German will continue to turn in his or her best with or without recognition, but Americans become disheartened and even resentful if they are not recognized. Not surprisingly, Germans find American compliments empty and insincere. "You did a good job on that report" is almost an insult to someone who regards doing a good job as normal. It's like being complimented for wearing matching socks.

In the dialogue, Cathy makes the mistake of judging German behavior by American standards. She has not received any positive feedback on her performance from her German supervisor, which in the feel-good, compliment-happy American workplace means she must not be doing very well. But in the German workplace, the absence of comment merely means Cathy is in fact meeting the rather high expectations Germans normally set for their employees, which is why Irmgard wonders what Cathy is worried about.

The German attitude toward compliments, or any kind of encouragement for that matter, is in large part a function of German perfectionism. Germans are especially intolerant of inefficiency, errors, mistakes, or snafus—anything that suggests a lack of discipline or vigilance. An untidy work space, for example, or a leaking faucet in the cafeteria or an improperly completed time sheet—all of these will draw an immediate rebuke. There is never an excuse for sloppiness, whether physical or mental. The Germans pride themselves on the efficiency of their systems—and, not surprisingly, they have systems for virtually everything—and spend more time and effort on training their workers than any country in Europe. In a country where people expect perfection more or less as a matter of course, the threshold for compliments is going to be rather high. To put it another way, if you're not getting complimented, it probably means you're doing a good job.

Perfectionism aside, there may be another factor at work here, the notion that the motivation to do a good job should come from within, that a person shouldn't need to be encouraged or recognized by someone else in order to do his or her best. You should naturally want to do your best, and your reward is the satisfaction you feel for having done so. "Praise of performance is rarely used to motivate employees [in Germany]," Greg Nees has observed,

> as is typical in the United States. Because of their thorough educational and vocational training, combined with their strong sense of accountability, Germans have internalized performance criteria and are highly self-directed.... The more emotional motivational strategies used by American managers are viewed as unnecessary hand-holding.
>
> Both employees and managers take the old Swabian saying *Net g'schimpft isch Lob g'nug* (If you weren't criticized, that's praise enough) quite literally. (2000, 105, 106)

For Americans, the need for recognition is partly a result of a certain national insecurity. They lack confidence in themselves in a way seldom seen among Europeans and require reassurance of their worth. On the surface this might seem backwards; with all the opportunity and wealth and their international preeminence—Americans more or less saved Europe from Hitler, after all, and then rebuilt it—Americans ought to be *more* confident than Europeans, not less. In a perverse sort of way, however, it may be their very success that causes Americans to doubt themselves. When success comes easily, when there appear to be no real limits to what one can accomplish, nothing external that is holding one back, then there's bound to be some doubt that whatever someone has achieved, he or she could always have achieved more. If the only limits to success are internal, then in a perverse kind of way the very act of achieving a certain degree of success only reminds a person of his or her inadequacies. "In America," Stuart Miller has observed, "it is especially hard nowadays to have personal pride. The doors of opportunity in our country are, supposedly, open to all. Therefore, one is always inclined to question oneself and ask why one isn't rich and famous, or richer and *more* famous" (1990, 62, 63).

Another factor here may be that Americans have always tended to find their identity in things external to themselves, to find validation in their possessions, for example, and especially in their achievements—in the things they've done, the people they know, the places they've been. This is a large part of an American's identity. It should not be surprising, therefore, that Americans would look to compliments from others, yet another kind of external reinforcement, to strengthen their sense of self-worth.

42. Surprise

Michael is not the man to be making the case for Herr Schmidt. Ostensibly extolling Schmidt's virtues, he seems, rather, to be reading from a list of Ten Ways Not to Succeed in Germany. Each of the "strengths" he mentions (Schmidt's an "original," he's "not afraid to bend the rules," he will "shake things up," he "will surprise us") are in fact liabilities from the German point of view. And the one liability that Heidi mentions (he's "unpredictable"), Michael takes to be a strength. Michael has a few things to learn about Germans.

To begin with, Schmidt is an original—in a culture, don't forget, that values conformity. Originality disconcerts the Germans and makes them anxious; it smacks too much of the unknown and the uncertain. Germans prefer people who are like everyone else, people who fit the mold as opposed to being one of a kind. People who stand out too much or are otherwise different can't be relied on or trusted to do the right thing. They might cause embarrassment. It's probably no accident that while England, France, and the United States all have the tradition of the lovable eccentric who adds color to life, Germany does not. Lovable and eccentric don't go together in the German mind. This doesn't mean, by the way, that Germans don't admire people who are inventive or creative, for they admire that kind of originality very much. They just want such people to act like the rest of us when they're in public.

Far worse, of course, is the fact that Schmidt is apparently willing to "bend the rules." Rules are the glue that holds society together, without which there is chaos—and so far as Germans are concerned, knowing and obeying the rules are very close to the greatest good. After all, anything that undermines the rules or anyone who disregards them is a threat to order. And order, of course, *is* the greatest good. John Mole writes of the "panoply of regulations" in the German business world. "It may not be the most regulated business environment in Europe," he adds,

> but it is certainly the one in which regulations are most adhered to. In addition to regulations there are a host of guidelines and principles covering every aspect of running a business. In the unlikely event that a loophole is discovered, it is customary not to exploit it but to refer to the appropriate authority for a ruling. (1995, 30)

Then there's the fact that Schmidt is unpredictable, to which Michael adds approvingly that he is "someone who will surprise us." If Heidi was in doubt about Schmidt before this, now she must be genuinely alarmed. We noted earlier (Dialogue 35, "Shortcut," page 185) how the Germans like to avoid uncertainty and the unknown, which means, of course, that anyone who is unpredictable is therefore automatically suspect. By the same logic, Germans also do not like to be surprised and have gone to great lengths—all their laws, procedures, and elaborate systems—to minimize the unexpected. Germans like to anticipate whatever can be anticipated; they like to be ready. To most Germans a "pleasant surprise" is an oxymoron.

Americans absorb what is new and different—the unknown and the unexpected—much more readily than the average European does. Americans are quite comfortable with change—the looming shake-up in marketing wouldn't ruffle as many feathers in the United States—and much less in awe of tradition. In Europe what is new must be proven to be better (not always an easy task), whereas in the U.S. what is new is assumed to be better (whether it is in fact or not). As for rules, if they are not actually made to be broken, they are certainly nothing more than works in progress. And what is original is more likely to be met with curiosity and genuine interest than with anxiety or suspicion.

Why do Americans so readily embrace all of these alarming qualities? Why are phenomena like experimentation, breaking the mold, a new paradigm, and changing the way we do things around here such good things in the American lexicon? Because Americans can't help themselves (no more, of course, than Germans can help being the way they are). As noted earlier, America was the New World, full of surprises, teeming with the unpredictable, shot through with the uncertain, the unknown, and the unexpected—a typical German's worst nightmare. To survive you had to let go of the old ways, or if not let go, then at least adapt them to fit the new circumstances. But in many cases, of course, those circumstances—the environment, the living conditions, the tasks people faced—were completely unprecedented. Whether early Americans were culturally inclined to "shake things up" (to use Michael's phrase from the dialogue) didn't really matter; things were already shaken up for them.

The German national experience has been the story of the struggle for stability, to fashion some kind of order and structure out of nearly two hundred years of political conflict and economic disruption, what Richard Lord calls "the ups, downs, spins, turnarounds, and collapses" of German history (1996, 39). Nor do you need a long memory to recall Germany's instability; some of the worst that history had to offer took place in the early and mid-twentieth century, with the collapse of the Weimar Republic and the two world wars. The Germans have had enough of change and long for stasis; they cling to the known, the certain, and the safe. This is not exactly the creed of the entrepreneur, of course, and is an attitude that often catches American business types off guard, but it is understandable under the circumstances. It should be noted, however, that even Germans know this craving for security is not always good for business. "We need an entirely different approach to life," one German entrepreneur recently complained.

> People are paralyzed with their fear of change in Germany. Nobody dares to take any risks. Unless we find a way to encourage greater initiative, we are heading for a lot of trouble in the 21st century.... You do not want to take a chance with failure because in Germany, unlike in the United States, there are rarely any second chances. (Drozdiak 1998, Sec. A13)

43. Thinking on Your Feet

Alice has certainly pushed some German buttons in this dialogue. She no doubt feels that so long as the basics are in place in the training design, what can it hurt to have to improvise the Bosch presentation a bit here and there? Improvising, however, whether at the core or the periphery, rubs Germans the wrong way. This is why Helga's immediate response to the news that Alice hasn't finished the design yet is to try to reschedule the presentation. For Helga, no presentation is preferable to an incomplete one. When Alice misses this cue and insists on going ahead as planned, Helga tries to stop her again ("Improvise?"), but

Alice thinks it's just a language problem and defines the word ("You know, think on our feet").

But the problem here is not with the vocabulary; it's with the whole concept. Germans tend to believe that whatever can go wrong, will, and they are therefore distinctly uncomfortable with spontaneity, with anything done on the spur of the moment. By definition such things cannot have been thought through, and anything that hasn't been thought through, from every angle, cannot be trusted or relied on. People shouldn't do their thinking on their feet, in other words; they should do it ahead of time, sitting down. Writing about the task of integrating East Germany into the former West Germany, John Ardagh notes,

> Germans may be excellent at routine methodical work, but they have little flair for improvisation or innovation; yet this is just what the problems of the east have needed. There are no set rules, of the kind Germans love, for the unprecedented challenge of converting a country and its economy from Communism to the free market. In short, west Germans have the wealth for the job, but not the aptitude. (1995, 6)

Improvising reeks of risk and of being undisciplined and disorganized, all very alarming concepts for the typical German. It also means having to rely on one's instincts as opposed to one's intellect, an even more disturbing prospect. Worst of all, improvising is the very opposite of planning; and planning, for reasons touched on elsewhere in this chapter, is quite high on the German list of Good Things. Not to plan is bad enough, of course, but to reveal your lack of planning to others, which is always the danger when you have to improvise, is much worse. To appear unprepared before a client or customer is simply unprofessional. As painful as it will be, and it will not be much fun, Helga will call Bosch and postpone the meeting.

For their part, Americans have been making it up as they go along from the very beginning. Improvising, flying by the seat of one's pants, playing it by ear—whatever it's called, Americans can handle spontaneity. The American national experience was one encounter after another with the unexpected; those who couldn't improvise didn't survive. This attitude is not easy for Europeans to understand, perhaps because theirs is a much more "finished" culture compared with the work in progress the United States represents. "Of this necessity to invent brand-new solutions for brand-new problems," Luigi Barzini has observed, "Europeans are not fully aware. Many of them tenaciously cling to the belief that most situations, no matter how unprecedented, can be better understood, and problems solved, if reduced to terms familiar to their own great-grandfathers" (1983, 220).

It's not that Americans think people should go out of their way to improvise—they don't *prefer* it to planning and being prepared—it's just that it doesn't bother or frighten them. Indeed, Americans greatly admire people who can think on their feet, and they also believe that planning can be carried too far. The danger, as they see it, is that if you plan too carefully, you become a prisoner of your plan and run the risk of losing your flexibility, the ability to throw your plan out when the unexpected happens. And—and this is the point—no matter how much you plan, something unexpected always does happen, which is where the Germans would disagree; for them, planning can actually *prevent* the unexpected from happening.

The recent DaimlerChrysler merger will no doubt prove a rich laboratory for observing this and other German-American cultural differences. A *Newsweek* article on the new company has noted that

> Americans favor fast-paced trial-and-error experimentation; Germans lay painstaking plans and implement them precisely. "The Americans think the Germans are stubborn militarists, and the Germans think the Americans are totally chaotic," says Edith Meissner, an executive at the Sindelfingen plant. To foster compromise, Americans are encouraged to make more specific plans, and Germans are urged to begin experimenting more quickly. (McGinn and Theil 1999, 51, 52)

44. Rude

What people consider rude behavior in any given situation depends very much on what they consider polite behavior for that same situation. If it's considered polite to shake hands with people when they come into the room, for example, and you neglect to do so, then you are rude. But if it's polite not to shake hands, and you do, then once again you're rude. Rudeness is simply the absence or opposite of whatever is polite.

As we have noted elsewhere, Germans feel strongly that people should obey the rules, that awareness of and adherence to a common set of behaviors is what guarantees the social order. Conformity, therefore, is a key German value. When people do not conform, when they transgress social norms, Germans feel it is important and appropriate to point this out, in part because they assume the transgressor would be grateful to know about the mistake or oversight and eager to correct it, and in part because it is simply one's civic responsibility to make sure rules are being followed, whether transgressors appreciate it or not.

"There is a strong sense of community and social conscience," John Mole has observed,

> which to some may appear based more on social tidiness than genuine neighborliness.... Eccentricity of the mildest sort will attract open criticism. While there is an instinctive dislike of personal confrontation, there is no hesitation in pointing out to someone that he or she does not meet acceptable standards of behavior. This may be for something as trivial, in your eyes, as taking off a jacket at a meeting or parking in the wrong place. Policing each other's behavior is not seen as offensive but as a social duty. (1995, 40)

Americans, on the other hand, are a tolerant and largely nonconforming people; they can live with diversity of views and behaviors. They understand that people can arrive at the same place via different paths and that on occasion people may stray from the straight and narrow. Indeed, the rebel or nonconformist, the man or woman who defies prevailing sentiment and charts his or her own course, is a prototypical American hero. More important, perhaps, is the fact that Americans are loath to trod upon the personal freedom of others and will go out of their way to allow people their harmless idiosyncrasies (somewhat of an oxymoron in Germany). You will be much more readily—and heartily—condemned in the United States for usurping someone's individual liberty than you will be for indulging their peccadilloes. The social order is strong enough to accommodate a dash of deviancy.

It's not surprising, then, that Todd finds Dieter rude—and that Elke doesn't understand why. From Todd's point of view, Dieter is intruding on something that's none of his business. But in Germany how Todd's desk looks *would* be another person's business, in the sense that everyone has a responsibility to make sure everyone else respects basic social norms. Indeed, a convincing case could be made that *not* saying anything to Todd about his messy office would be rude, or at least inconsiderate. Coincidentally, the particular transgression on display here, untidiness, is especially offensive to Germans, whose passion for order makes neatness, particularly in public places, a high priority. One final point to consider here is the fact that in this particular case Dieter is right: a messy desk does make it look bad when people visit. And for Germans, being right *in and of itself* gives you the justification to say something, whether it's rude or not.

It's true, incidentally, that even in the United States Dieter would probably be forgiven for criticizing Todd if he were the receptionist, let's say, whose work space was part of visitors' first impression. But Todd would be quite justified in expecting to be left alone back in his office or cubicle, out of the public eye. It may be, moreover, that even in his own country Todd's untidiness won't earn him any points with management, that he may pay a price for the freedom to be messy, but in the U.S. that's Todd's problem, not Dieter's. And certainly not society's.

Americans come by their tolerance honestly enough. From the beginning, theirs was a country of commingled cultures, once known as the melting pot, including the British, Dutch, Germans, and Scandinavians, to mention just a few nationalities. If people didn't somehow figure out how to make peace with those who had entirely different views and traditions, to let them be, then they didn't prosper in the young country. Americans long ago agreed to disagree on all but the most important things, and the most important of those important things was the right to be different. "Don't tread on me" was inscribed on one of the first flags in colonial America, and while the overtones were political rather than personal, the phrase accurately reflected the American tradition of tolerance. Over time another phrase came along to express the same sentiment, a phrase not likely to be heard in Germany: "Live and let live."

45. Closing Costs

Many American companies have what might best be called an opportunistic relationship with the communities in which they are located. They stay in the community so long as it serves their purposes, and when it no longer does, they leave. And everybody understands. There might be some ritual hand-wringing, but in the end people realize this is how business works, with its eye on the bottom line. It should be remembered, of course, that communities, or at least the employees who live in them, have a similarly opportunistic relationship with their companies; when an employee finds a better job elsewhere, he or she takes it. And the company understands.

John Mole has written that

> a characteristic of American corporate life is constant upheaval in which social hierarchies and relationships are repeatedly disturbed.
>
> Organisations exist independently of their members. The needs of individuals are seen as subsid-

iary to the needs of the organisation.... The readiness of companies to fire surplus or underperforming employees and the corresponding readiness of employees to change companies in order to further a career are part of an arm's-length relationship between an individual and an organisation. While the immediate feelings of "terminated" employees may be as bruised as those of a European counterpart...it is accepted as the way things work. If the organisation's needs change again, those people may be hired back into the company at a later date. (1995, 154)

By and large, German corporations define their social responsibilities more broadly and take them more seriously. They have a much closer relationship with their communities; in fact, the ultimate aim of business is to serve society, which means that the relationship with the community does not depend entirely on the bottom line. To put it another way, for German companies the bottom line *is* the relationship with the community. So it is, as Hannah is trying to suggest in the dialogue, that when businesses make decisions, they should always consider the impact of their actions on the welfare of the community. When a large German housing construction company failed a few years ago, jeopardizing the jobs of two thousand skilled laborers, Chancellor Kohl publicly appealed to its creditors to remember "their responsibilities...[to all] the skilled tradesmen affected," suggesting that the plight of the newly unemployed workers should be the concern of the wider community and not just the tradesmen themselves (Atkinson 1994, D1). If this happened in the United States, the out-of-work tradesmen would be quite surprised to learn that someone else was responsible for them; they would just start scrambling to find new jobs.

"Germany's underlying ethic of social responsibility," Greg Nees observes,

> is directly related to the German sense of duty, which is manifested in a company's obligation to do more than simply produce goods and services. Traditionally, American and British public companies have existed to maximize return on investment for their shareholders. As in other European countries, German public companies are expected to balance the interests of their shareholders with those of their workers and the common good of the community.
>
> [German] companies have strong ties with their local community and a clear sense of social responsibility, particularly for providing lifetime jobs for their employees.... This strong attitude toward creating and maintaining long-term employment underpins the social market ethic that places a high premium on company loyalty. (2000, 98, 102, 103)

In the dialogue Paul, the American, finds himself faced with a fairly straightforward business decision: production at the Freiburg plant is last again; the plant should therefore be closed. Indeed, given the recent flight of two other manufacturing companies from Freiburg, Paul now sees that he "probably should have acted faster" and closed the plant some time ago. He is heartened to see that his colleague Hannah agrees with him, judging from her remark that "the plant's really too small to be efficient anymore."

But there's a good chance Hannah does not agree, which Paul would see if he could only construe her words

from a more German point of view. Hannah *does* agree
that the plant is inefficient, as she herself says, but for
Germans inefficiency in and of itself would not necessarily justify closing a plant. Other factors would have to be
taken into consideration, such as the impact on the workers and the town, which seems to be what Hannah is getting at in her next remark, that the plant has "lasted…more
than fifty years." While Paul takes this to mean that the
plant is outdated and overdue for closing, Hannah may be
suggesting that after fifty years of doing business in Freiburg,
the company has incurred certain obligations to the community. Any doubt that this is what she means is cleared
up by her next remark, that the other two major employers in the town pulled out three years ago and theirs is
"the only manufacturing plant left there now." Paul mis-
interprets again, thinking Hannah means their company
should have gotten out sooner, but what she probably
means is that now that they're the only major employer
left, it would be irresponsible for the company to close the
Freiburg operation.

Hannah knows, incidentally, that it might not make
economic sense to stay on in Freiburg, which is obviously
Paul's only criteria, but she's also concerned about whether
or not it makes social sense; at the very least, the social
repercussions should be examined. For the record Hannah's
point about the multinationals is not what Paul thinks it is,
that they have set some kind of example to be emulated.
On the contrary, they have behaved precisely as one would
expect a multinational to behave: a corporation that has no
nation to look out for or any particular society to feel obliged
to; they have acted exclusively on the basis of what was best
for the corporation. That might be good enough for a multinational but not for any self-respecting German company.

What accounts for such different views of the role of the company in society? Why is profit the bottom line in the United States and social responsibility most important in Germany? Part of the answer has to do with the source of capital in the two countries. As noted earlier (Dialogue 39, "Quality," page 187), in the U.S. the source of capital is primarily stockholders. If you make stockholders happy, you stay in business, and nothing makes stockholders happier than profits. No one would object, of course, if you were able to serve society *and* reward investors, but if you should ever have to choose, it shouldn't be difficult. Many Americans would probably add that there's really no conflict here, for keeping stockholders happy—by staying in business—*is* serving society.

The source of German capital is more likely to be central banks, which can afford to take a more long-term view of business. This in turn gives companies more time to develop profits and the freedom to serve other goals, such as the needs of society and the community. There may also be the feeling that because the central banks get their money from the general public, it is only proper that the public expect the companies to have a social conscience.

Another explanation, no doubt, is the mobility factor cited often in these pages. Where opportunity abounds (whether in fact or in myth), people are accustomed to chasing after it, and their roots don't go very deep. More than half of all Americans live more than fifty miles from where they grew up; the average house in the United States changes hands every seven years; and the average American changes jobs eight times in his or her career. In a country where people change communities this often, it's no surprise companies don't develop a loyalty to place.

By contrast, Germans are much more likely to stay put.

The people who work in your company are likely to be lifelong inhabitants of the community, perhaps even the second or third generation of family members to have worked in your employ. They aren't people who came from somewhere else chasing opportunity, nor are they liable to be going off on their own quest. Such a workforce means the company's roots are much more deeply planted in the community, with whose welfare, naturally, the company is bound to identify more closely. In such a world, it's not a matter of choosing between the interests of the company and the well-being of society, for they are virtually one and the same.

An American executive, in a famous formulation, allowed as how "What's good for GM (General Motors) is good for America." While Germans would certainly agree with the underlying premise of the symbiotic relationship between business and society, they would be inclined to turn the proposition around: What's good for society is good for BMW.

46. Team Leader

The Germans are a serious people and appreciate the trait in others. It's not that they never laugh or that they lack humor, but in the broader sense that they take life seriously and think deeply about it. The great French novelist Stendhal believed that "more witticisms are bandied about in Paris in one single evening than in all Germany in a month" (in Barzini 1983, 71). Germans believe it's important to understand what life is all about, and they are not afraid of tackling the big questions head-on. Indeed, they revel in it. It's no coincidence that so many of the greatest philosophers were German, towering figures such as Kant,

Heidegger, Hegel, Nietzsche, and Schopenhauer. Among Germans, John Ardagh has observed, "[n]ot to worry and be gloomy is not to be taken seriously as a thinker" (1995, 561).

Like any nationality, Germans find some subjects and some settings more appropriate for humor than others. "Among friends," Ardagh continues,

> [Germans] are lively and good fun, especially Berliners and Rhinelanders. But to be frivolous or ironic about serious or important subjects, in the British or French manner, can still make them uneasy.... Around a dinner table, there can be plenty of animated jokey conversation on personal matters, and then, if someone mentions a serious topic, the tone changes and lengthy debate ensues. And once a German gets his teeth into a subject of this kind, he likes to worry at it for hours. (1995, xiii)

German seriousness manifests itself in many ways. Germans tend to be intellectual, valuing knowledge for its own sake, and expect people to take a keen interest in ideas and to be able to hold their own in serious conversation. They admire people who are thoughtful, well-read, and well-spoken and have a relatively low tolerance for that which is superficial and shallow. They believe that there is a place for humor—and a number of other places where humor has no place whatsoever. They are not at all inclined to laugh at themselves. None of this means Germans don't like to have fun or enjoy life, but it does mean that for them, merely to enjoy life is not to reach very high. Beyond enjoying life, one should try one's best to understand it. Among other things, this loftiness of purpose accounts at least in part for that deep earnestness that is so pervasive in the German character.

Germans appreciate seriousness wherever they find it, but they particularly appreciate it at the office. "Levity does not belong at the workplace," John Mole has observed.

> Like so many aspects of German life, humor is strictly compartmentalized. The more formal the occasion, the less humor is acceptable.
>
> Far from putting Germans at their ease, joking among strangers or new acquaintances often makes them feel uncomfortable. At meetings or presentations, while an American or a Briton might feel obliged to sprinkle speeches or presentations with jokes, or an Italian or Frenchman would indulge in occasional witticisms, a German remains consistently serious.
>
> Among close colleagues in private there is banter and joking. It is usually sharp and biting and directed towards incompetence, mistakes and nonconformity. It is rarely facetious, especially about money or business, and never self-deprecating. To admit inadequacy even in jest is incomprehensible. (1995, 42)

Americans are not an especially serious people and are in fact suspicious of anyone who is what they call "too serious" (a phrase that would never occur to a German). Americans aren't that concerned with getting to the bottom of things, figuring out what it all means. They don't quite see the point. If there were practical benefits to figuring things out, if knowing the meaning of life meant they could pick stocks better or drive further between oil changes, that would be another matter. As for ideas and knowledge, they're nice if you've got the time. In the final analysis, life is too short to be taken seriously.

For Americans nothing is beyond the reach of humor. Indeed, they like nothing better than stepping back from the human condition and laughing at it. What else can one do, after all? ("Figure it out," the Germans would say.) And if there's one thing Americans can't abide, it's people who are unable to laugh at themselves. Americans have a very keen nose for such people and have assigned them-selves the role of making them lighten up. This doesn't mean, incidentally, that Americans can't be serious or think deeply; one just has to show them the benefit of doing so.

In the dialogue the American, Pamela, is under the mistaken impression that she and Gerhard are making a case *against* Dr. Mueller as lead negotiator, listing his vari-ous liabilities. He's "very serious," "thinks deeply about things," and doesn't make jokes. These would be liabili-ties to many Americans, in the sense that they would not necessarily warm to such a person; they would prefer some-one more gregarious and less cerebral, someone who puts everyone at ease. But these same "liabilities" *would* put Germans at ease, of course, which is why Gerhard assumes he and Pamela are making the case *for* Dr. Mueller ("So you favor him too?").

Why aren't Americans more contemplative and philo-sophic, more serious? For one thing, they are people of action. There was always a great deal to be done in America, and that didn't leave much time for deep think-ing (or for poetry, painting, or music, for that matter). For another, Americans are a practical people; they identify with and gravitate toward the concrete, the immediate, and the utilitarian, which doesn't leave much of a cheer-ing section for deep thought. In the end, though, the real reason Americans are so indifferent to what it all means is probably their suspicion that nothing would change if they found out.

For their part, the German desire to figure everything out (the same impulse which makes them such good engineers) derives in part from that most German of all emotions: angst. *Angst* means anxiety, doubt, or a kind of non-specific uneasiness; it comes from not knowing, from that very uncertainty already identified as the bane of German existence. If only we could know how everything works and what everything means, then there would be no more uncertainty. And without uncertainty, there would be no more angst.

47. Misleading

German bluntness has been much remarked upon. While Americans are considered direct by most cultures of the world, Germans are one of the few nationalities Americans find more direct than they are. Most Germans would probably not dispute this characterization, though they would disagree strenuously that it was a criticism. Directness, after all, is a by-product of telling the truth, and there could never be anything wrong with the truth.

"Because Germans believe that content is more important than style," Roland Flamini has written,

> they can be brutally frank. Rarely is there anything to read between the lines and hardly ever is the conversation so subtle as to be open to more than one interpretation. The plus side of this trait is that they will never tell you something because they think it's what you want to hear. Varnishing the truth isn't a German trait, nor is it a trait they ap-

preciate in others. (1997, 69, 70)

Naturally, Germans have little patience with people who aren't equally plain speaking, which is what has gotten Frank into trouble in the dialogue. If Frank thought Helmut's report needed a lot of work, that's what he should have said; to say anything less is condescending and patronizing. And what if Frank was only trying not to hurt Helmut's feelings? Be serious, Germans would say, and give Helmut credit. He's a grown-up; he can handle the truth. "A number of German acquaintances...have told me that they don't really feel comfortable dealing with Americans," Richard Lord has observed.

> Why? Because they just can't trust them. What they mean with this put-down is that Americans...tend to be altogether more circumspect in their criticisms, that they will pad the truth to protect the other person's feelings. If this is your way of doing things, be aware that Germans don't see it as any kind of virtue. You are better advised to become a little more blunt in your pronouncements, to drop all the adornments of rhetorical airbrushing and serve up a more point-blank account of what you think and feel.... (1996, 50)

This is especially true in the situation in the dialogue, where Frank's failure to be forthright may undermine Helmut's performance and adversely affect his standing with his superiors. Gratuitous bluntness is one thing, and it is not appreciated even by Germans, but speaking plainly when it's for another person's own good will not only not be taken as a criticism, which is what Frank is afraid of, but will be seen as a sign of consideration. After all, if the truth hurts, it's hardly the fault of the truth teller. "[I]n terms of stating facts," Greg Nees says,

> offering criticism, and issuing direct commands, Germans are generally more direct [than Americans].... As mentioned earlier, directness and honesty are highly valued by Germans and thus among the most telling characteristics of their style of speech. Part of this emphasis on directness is related to their desire for Klarheit [clarity] and dislike of ambiguity. (2000, 72, 73)

From this perspective being critical is also a way to be socially responsible.

Europeans routinely remark that Americans worry too much about being liked and not enough about being respected, by which they seem to mean that Americans hedge when it comes to telling truths that might hurt or upset someone. For Germans, a true friend or colleague doesn't protect one from the truth but helps one see it. Indeed, someone who is less than candid out of fear of hurting another person's feelings is in the end only protecting her- or himself, not the other person. For Germans (and also the French), the operative word in the phrase "the truth hurts" is *truth*, not *hurts*.

48. Slow Going

Germans hate mistakes—and anything that contributes to making mistakes, such as doing things too fast, taking risks, being sloppy, or, in the language of the dialogue, taking shortcuts. They are, accordingly, great fans of anything that prevents or minimizes the possibility of mistakes, such as following procedures, being deliberate and methodical, refusing to be rushed or to compromise, and, above all, being thorough. The appeal of thoroughness, of course, is that it goes a long way toward guaranteeing the high quality that is so dear to the German heart.

"There is a pervasive commitment to doing things thoroughly," Richard Lord has written,

> a quality [foreigners] find, by turns, reassuring and irritating. Foreigners here frequently discover that Germans will come in and put the finishing touches on what [the foreigners] thought they had already completed in a fairly decent manner. Or the Germans will tell them that the job has been done well so far—now complete it. (1996, 48–49)

In short, Germans never do things by halves. If they can't do a thing properly, if the only way to get something done is to rush it through, then they won't attempt it at all. If they're not sure their product is as good as they can make it, for example, if they have not checked and rechecked it for every possible flaw or error, then they feel they must continue checking it, no matter how long it takes, and no one will fault them for doing so. On the other hand, if they stop testing or checking before everything is as it should be, to beat the competition to the market, for example, then they will have earned the opprobrium that will surely be heaped upon them.

This thoroughness is in part simply fallout from the German fixation on perfection. "Prior to a launch," Roland Flamini has observed,

> market and product testing can sometimes be carried to extremes. At the main Mercedes-Benz plant in Stuttgart, visitors are proudly shown the testing

rooms where the doors of a vehicle are hydrauli-
cally slammed shut and reopened again and again
for days, until the door finally falls off its hinges.
The number of openings and closings is meticu-
lously recorded and compared with previous door
slammings to ensure that the component has lost
none if its toughness. (1997, 41)

This is the logic Carol has come up against in the dialogue. She's worried about getting the new design into production so that her company can compete with Feuer. If
Carol and Brigid's company doesn't have a product on the
shelves at the same time or before Feuer, Carol believes,
regardless of the quality, then their company can't compete. Brigid, on the other hand, believes that without quality they can't compete anyway—whether or not they've
got a product on the shelves. Not surprisingly, Carol's remark that Feuer will have its new widget in the stores in
six weeks doesn't phase Brigid, who knows that guaranteeing quality takes time. Indeed, her response, "They must
have started before we did. Or else they've got more people
working on it," is Brigid's way of saying that if Feuer is
indeed beating their company to the market, it's not because Feuer has compromised on thoroughness. And neither should they!

Carol misses (or ignores) this, continuing to push the
theme that product review takes "too long." Brigid makes
the case for German perfectionism one last time ("Our
engineers don't miss much, that's for sure") but gets nowhere, judging from Carol's response that she intends to
ask Herr Neuger to look for shortcuts in the process. As
the camera pulls back, Carol and Brigid are surely walking
away shaking their heads, Carol amazed that German companies ever make a profit given their obsession with de-

tail, Brigid wondering if Americans honestly think there can be shortcuts to perfection.

The point of this dialogue is not to suggest that American companies don't care about quality or that German companies don't worry about time-to-market. It's more a question of degree, as is often the case with cultural differences. When push comes to shove, Americans might be more likely to compromise on quality in favor of efficiency, while Germans would sacrifice almost anything before they would jeopardize quality.

In casting about for an explanation, we are reminded yet again of the European fear of failure and the related reluctance to take risks. Europeans are much more threatened by the possibility of failure than are Americans, and since failure is inherent in risk, they are likewise much more risk-averse. If being thorough and detail-oriented in the extreme can prevent failure, then the time that takes seems a small price to pay.

A related theme here is surely the relative lack of mobility in Europe, alluded to earlier. If people can't run away from their failures and the long memories they engender in others, then they're bound to be more cautious and conservative. There is also in Europe a general sense that life doesn't offer up that many opportunities and virtually no second chances; to waste an opportunity, therefore, is especially reckless. Needless to say, the German obsession with perfection may be grounded in these same two phenomena.

Finally, the flexibility and freedom that German businesses enjoy because banks, not stockholders, are the primary source of investment capital mean they have no good reason *not* to indulge their penchant for thoroughness. They would probably do so anyway, but they wouldn't be nearly so calm about it.

Americans, as noted frequently, have a more casual attitude about things. They're pragmatists, after all; they know that everything can't be perfect and that there is an inherent unpredictability to life. Germans know this, too— it drives them crazy, in fact—but rather than accept the unpredictable, they try to eliminate it. Mistakes happen, and you learn from them. You should always do your best, of course, when you're designing a product: planning for contingencies, testing and retesting, perfecting anything you can. And then you take a deep breath. There's a limit to how thorough you can be, a point of diminishing returns beyond which thoroughness is little more than self-indulgence. You don't deliberately make mistakes, but you know they sometimes happen. We're only human, after all, and humans get things wrong on occasion. (Germans would agree, of course, but it's a problem they're definitely working on.)

Edward Stewart and Milton Bennett have observed how most Europeans feel that "solutions should be attempted only after the problem is thoroughly understood. Americans are far more likely to engage in trial-and-error solutions, actions which earn them the label of 'impetuous,' both in foreign relations and interpersonal encounters" (1991, 155). In point of fact that kind of thoroughness and striving for perfection were simply not possible in the New World; there evolved, instead, the philosophy of "good enough" or "making do," which has survived to some extent down to the present day. The scale of many of the tasks facing early immigrants was such that very often the question was not so much whether the job could be done well but whether it could be done at all. When the deadline for planting arrived, for example, people didn't worry about the unsightly stumps in their newly cleared fields; they either planted their seeds or didn't eat in the winter. In Germany, by contrast, where the fields have been cleared for centuries, farmers are free to indulge their passion for perfection. Thus it is that the pragmatic streak in the American national character, which Europeans sometimes interpret as laziness or having low standards, may in fact have a rather respectable pedigree.

49. A Hunch

By and large Americans trust their instincts. They have a deep—Germans would say naive—faith in their hunches, their gut reactions, their intuitions. Americans think that instincts are somehow pure until they get corrupted and spoiled by too much analysis and thinking. They believe that if they act on their instincts, on what their feelings tell them, they are almost never wrong. On the other hand, they feel that if they act after lengthy discussion and overanalysis, after too much calculation and second guessing (if that can still be called "acting"), they may or may not get it right.

Germans would beg to disagree. In their view, they would do just as well to base judgments on sheep entrails as on hunches and intuitions. It's not that Germans have anything against feelings or emotions—they are, in fact, a deeply romantic and sentimental people—but only that intuition has no place in business decision making.

What should decisions be based on, then? On the facts, of course, on data, scientific evidence, and any other objective measures at hand, on reason and logic, on the products of the mind, on the truth, on anything *except* feelings and intuitions. Germans believe in the power of the mind, in the ability of the intellect to analyze reality and discover the truth. They place great reliance on experts, for example, and on objective, rational investigation. "It would be difficult," Greg Nees writes,

> to overestimate the German respect for understanding based on rational analysis and scientific knowledge, both of which are seen as ways of creating Klarheit [clarity].
>
> Germans also desire clear, unambiguous knowledge as a way to reduce the general insecurity and anxiety that plague them, since having knowledge is one of the best forms of control. From the German perspective, you can only control that which you understand, keeping ever-lurking chaos at bay. (2000, 54–55)

In the dialogue Greta tries to bring reason into the conversation when she asks Ralph if his decision is based on something he has read. She's clearly not comfortable acting on the basis of a vague, amorphous "something" that has apparently spoken to Ralph, a purely subjective phenomenon, in other words, with no discernible grounding in objective fact (or even in a second person's opinion). But if Ralph was acting on the basis of something he read, a study, perhaps, or some kind of research—on *anything* other than his own personal feelings—then that would be reassuring. Ralph doesn't sense Greta's concern and proceeds to confirm her worst suspicions when he says it actually is "just a hunch" he's got. To be absolutely sure (to give Ralph one last chance?), Greta asks him to reconfirm that what he's talking about is really nothing more than "a feeling." And Ralph obliges, uttering the dreaded words (to a German, anyway): "I can't really explain it." Anything that can't be explained, that by implication has not been thought through, must never be relied upon.

Americans have always set great store by what might be called subjective wisdom, the wisdom of personal experience, which is ultimately the source of their hunches and feelings. As a practical matter, they had little else but intuition to go on in the New World. It was all uncharted territory, both literally and figuratively. People had to do things they either had never done before or had never done in these circumstances. They could not know ahead of time what would work, nor did they have the luxury of assembling data and evidence before acting. There were no experts to rely on, no wise sages who could dispense the received wisdom. By definition any such wisdom would have to have been received from European thinkers and was for that very reason suspect, if not irrelevant. The only wisdom available was being created on the spot. "[T]he sheer novelty of American conditions," Daniel Boorstin writes,

> made useless much of the advice found in English books. It was remarkable that any progress had been made, Jared Eliot observed in 1748, "When we consider…the first Settlers…[were] coming from an old Cultivated Country to thick Woods [and] rough, unimproved Lands, where all their former Experience and Knowledge was now of very little service to them…." (1958, 263)

There was a lot of room, in other words, for relying on one's instincts, on one's best guess about what would work or what was true, on trusting what was self-evident. "[I]t was a way of thinking," Boorstin continues, "pervaded by doubt that the professional thinker could think better than others" and found its footing in the belief "that deep reflection does not necessarily produce the best action…" (151).

For their part, Germans have always believed that in the end if people are disciplined, methodical, and patient, they can always discover what is best without having to rely on hunches and educated guesses. Hunches are the refuge of the lazy and the impatient, and as for educated guesses, the truly educated never have to guess.

50. Hello Christian
51. Lunch at the Rathskeller

We conclude with two dialogues about the differences be-tween German and American social interaction, specifi-cally about the way individuals from the two cultures think of and establish relationships with other people. Ameri-cans tend to identify in a general way with humanity, look-ing "upon everyone they encounter as having the same basic nature as themselves," John McElroy has written, and believing "that human beings have certain wholesome interests in common. Smiling at a stranger reflects a view of strangers as potential friends" (1999, 212). There is a characteristic predisposition to like (and even to trust) strangers when one meets them and relatively little hesi-tation about making their acquaintance. Indeed, in the United States many people actually reach out to strang-ers, and even those who don't would not find it odd or alarming if a stranger approached and started speaking to them. Americans are an accessible people with a gener-ally inclusive attitude toward others, a predisposition in their favor, and a corresponding tradition of informal in-teractions.

This is not the case in Germany, or across most of Eu-rope for that matter. There is, rather, a tendency to distance oneself from the great mass of humanity and to identify only with select individuals, one's ingroup. "Europeans," Stuart Miller has noted, "try not to need new people" (1990, 44). The assumption made about strangers is not that they are more or less like us but that they probably would not make good company and that in any case until one knows for sure, usually through the medium of a third party, the safest thing is to stay away. There is a predisposition against strangers, in other words, and virtually no reaching out.

The natural instinct in Germany, therefore, is to keep one's distance from people one doesn't know, to prefer not to be approached, and in general to avoid casually adding to one's circle of acquaintances. Most interactions between people unknown to each other tend to be reserved and formal. The idea seems to be that while you can always warm up later to a person you initially kept at arm's length, it's rather more awkward to become cool toward someone you at first treated warmly. When two Germans meet, therefore, they do not assume they will eventually become acquaintances or friends; in fact, if they assume anything, it is that they will not.

Familiarity or intimacy is something Germans bestow upon each other, not something they presume. Out of politeness, therefore, when Germans make a new acquaintance, they maintain a certain formality and are much more likely to use last names and titles (though this is less true of the younger generation). Americans, on the other hand, like David in Dialogue 50, feel uncomfortable using last names and switch to first names almost immediately. Thus, while both Franz and Dr. Kuntsler address David by his last name and title (Dr. Wilson) and Franz likewise introduces his friend as Dr. Christian Kuntsler, David uses first names only (Franz and Christian) and leaves off the title. While David is only trying to be what he would no doubt call "friendly," his behavior will almost certainly seem too familiar to the two Germans. John Ardagh tells the story of a "seemingly cheerful clerical assistant [in an office in Hamburg who] suddenly killed herself; not a person in the firm knew anything at all about her life or had had any social contact with her, although she had been there for three years" (1995, 187).

More evidence of the inclusive/exclusive dichotomy can be found in the two versions of the pronoun *you* that are used in German (as well as French and many other European languages). This phenomenon permits German speakers to further signal and regulate the degree of familiarity they desire with another person. There is the formal version, *Sie*, when you want to suggest greater distance, and the more personal version, *du*, when you want to suggest less. Two Germans working in the same office might use *Sie* for months or even years with each other, only switching to *du* when they become close friends. Indeed, there used to be a formal ritual, called the *Bruderschaft*, to mark the changeover from *Sie* to *du*, the transition from acquaintance or colleague to intimate friend. The two friends would go to a bar, order a drink, entwine their arms, and drink out of each other's glass.

"Within the German home," Edward T. Hall and Mildred Reed Hall have written,

> family members abide by formal rules of behavior designed to give one another distance and privacy. These patterns of formality extend in adulthood to relations with friends and coworkers in the office. German friends of many years continue to address each other by their last names: "Herr

Schmidt," not "Walter." (1990, 39)

In Dialogue 51 we see another manifestation of this characteristic German *reserve* (the word Americans would use, but not Europeans): the rather stately pace at which relationships develop. In cultures where privacy is harder to come by (as in densely populated Europe), where it is something that has to be fought for and won, people have developed the habit of leaving each other alone. Since it's often not possible to get away from people, it becomes necessary to act as if they're not really there. In such cultures, the only way people get privacy is if they grant it to each other. Germans, like Otto in the dialogue, are therefore very sensitive about intruding or forcing themselves on other people. The new man, Hans, for example, who only started yesterday (and who actually works in another division), may not be ready to spend time with Otto and Ted, not ready to know them just yet or ready to be known by them. In any case, being German, Hans will understand if they do not approach him this early and will not think they're being distant and unfriendly. Indeed, in not approaching him prematurely, they are being polite and considerate. "For Americans," Greg Nees writes,

> accustomed to meeting strangers and being welcomed openly by them, the German formality and aloofness may seem cold and unfriendly. For Germans, on the other hand, it is being friendly toward strangers that is seen as unusual—and not necessarily positive. Whereas Americans often equate formality with unfriendliness and lack of ease, Germans have been raised to view reserve and formality as the proper signs of respect for people they don't know well. (2000, 46, 47)

Part of the explanation for this cultural difference is no doubt the fact that Germans change jobs and move much less often than do Americans. There's a good chance that the people who come into a German's life will be there for quite some time, and there is no urgency, therefore, about getting to know them. Nor do Germans expect they're going to become friends with every new hire in their department. In fact the typical German makes very few friends (as opposed to what the Germans call acquaintances) in the course of his or her life, often no more than two or three, though these friendships tend to be deep and lasting. It's quite likely, then, that Hans and Otto are not going to become lifelong friends, which is another reason there's no need to invite Hans to lunch on his second day at work. Finally, there is the fact that Germans, unlike Americans, tend not to socialize with people from their workplace and in fact prefer to keep their work and private lives separate.

History also contains clues to German and American social patterns. For their part, early Americans *had* to reach out to people they didn't know, whether they were culturally inclined to or not. When people immigrate to a new land, to a place where everyone is a stranger, they don't have the luxury of keeping others at a distance. Nor did early Americans have to worry about privacy; in the seventeenth and eighteenth centuries, at least, the problem wasn't how to protect your privacy but how to find companionship. "The loneliness of life on the frontier and in rural, post-frontier America," McElroy has observed, "led Americans to value friendliness" (1999, 211).

The same impulse has helped make Americans a generally trusting people who naturally assume that others wish them well. And evidence of this openness of spirit can be found at every turn: in the way Americans smile and greet strangers in the street, in elevators, and in all manner of public places; in the honesty and directness of their speech, which is notably free of dissembling and evasion; in the ease and speed with which they invite other people into their homes (and show them all around); and even in their architecture, in houses with front porches and yards open to the street. Their lives, like their innermost thoughts and feelings, are open for everyone to see. Americans seemingly have nothing to hide and lack even the capacity for concealment.

"The most amazing feature of American life," the Swiss psychologist Carl Jung wrote,

> is its boundless publicity. Everybody has to meet everybody, and they even seem to enjoy this enormity. To a central European such as I am, this American publicity of life, the lack of distance between people, the absence of hedges or fences round the gardens...the open doors in the houses (one can look from the street right through the sitting-room and the adjoining bedroom into the backyard and beyond)...all this is more than disgusting; it is positively terrifying. (in Yapp 1988, 852)

Terrifying because it is so much the opposite of the closed, defensive habits of many Europeans, the product of centuries of warfare, pestilence, and upheaval.

As noted before in these pages, population density is another important influence on patterns of social interaction. Germany has 620 people per square mile, or more than eight times the population density of the United States; where people are numerous, other people are automatic competition for scarce land, limited resources, and generally fewer opportunities. In the U.S., where there was a superabundance of land and opportunity, the stranger was never such a threat. "Strangers are welcome," Benjamin Franklin wrote, "because there is room enough for them all, and, therefore, the old Inhabitants are not jealous of them" (Boorstin 1958, 194).

The class system in Europe may also have dictated a certain caution and formality in interacting with others; one did not want to inadvertently push oneself on one's betters or mistakenly mingle with those beneath one's station. In the United States, where everyone was equal (or almost so), where there were no class distinctions in the European sense, such mistakes were not possible. Finally, Ardagh thinks the German "fondness for titles [relates to] their need for categorising people which brings the security of Ordnung [basic law]. Though it may be changing with the younger generation, this remains a rather formal society, preferring formal codes of address and judging by appearances" (1995, 181).

Epilogue

Europe has what we do not have yet, a sense of the mysterious and inexorable limits of life...and we Americans have what they sorely need: a sense of life's possibilities.

—James Baldwin
Nobody Knows My Name

For the most part it has not been our purpose in these pages to describe how Americans and Europeans feel about each other—what Americans think of the French, for example, or how Germans view Americans. While we have on occasion noted how Americans are perceived by Europeans because of a particular cultural difference, and vice versa, we have by and large confined our efforts to presenting cultural differences (in the dialogues) and then explaining the differences and where they come from (in the analyses).

If we have ignored cultural characterizations, it is not because the attitudes of Europeans and Americans toward each other aren't important but only because they are not themselves the source of misunderstanding or confusion. The attitudes aren't the problem, in other words; the cultural differences are. And if the differences are explained, as attempted in these pages, then the attitudes will take care of themselves (in a perfect world, anyway). Moreover, while attitudes are partly the result of cultural differences, they are also the result of numerous other factors—historical, economic, political—that take us far afield from the realm of culture. Nevertheless, how these two groups feel about each other clearly affects what happens when Europeans and Americans come together and thus deserves a few minutes of our time in these closing pages.

Europeans' Attitudes toward Americans

One suspects that deep down Europeans would prefer not to have to take America seriously. Or even think about it. From the European point of view, America is not a country with any legitimate claims to seriousness; there are no great thinkers or philosophers, after all; no real intellectual life: very little art, music, or literature of note; and only the rudiments of sophistication and taste. And as if that weren't bad enough, America is also a country where the common man, of all people, sets the standard. Normally, then, no self-respecting European would pay any attention to such a place, but that's not really an option. The United States is such an economic, military, and geopolitical colossus, it's simply not possible to ignore it. Hence that air of exasperation and resignation one senses whenever a European is obliged to deal with Americans yet again.

In point of fact, Europeans' attitudes toward Americans are somewhat more complicated than this. Europeans are actually quite conflicted in their feelings about America, swinging from grudging admiration and envy on the one hand to impatience and utter disdain on the other. They much admire the dynamism and can-do attitude of Americans, for example, the sense of opportunity and possibility, but they can't help bemoaning what they consider the typical American's lack of depth and manners. At a recent executive training seminar in Lausanne, the European managers in attendance exhibited the usual mixture of admiration and disdain for Americans, according to *The Wall Street Journal*.

> Many expressed envy of American technology, entrepreneurial spirit, productivity and everything to do with the Internet revolution; but they also spoke disparagingly of American businessmen. Among their chief putdowns: Americans are provincial, ignorant of world affairs, uncouth, and too materialistic.
>
> "They admire the financial results of many American companies," [one participant noted] but when they meet managers from the U.S. they see that even the educated, affluent Americans "don't speak any language besides English, don't know how or when to eat and drink properly, and don't know anything about European history, let alone geography. Then they ask themselves 'How can they be beating us?'" (Hymowitz 2000, B1)

Some nineteenth-century European visitors, quoted in Richard Pells' *Not Like Us*, found America "dangerous, uncivilized, even barbaric...a nightmare threatening to obliterate all respect for tradition [and] culture" (1997, 4, 5). And, in the next breath, they found the same country "a new Eden [with] a promise of redemption for the common folk" (5). Then and now, Pells continues, "The European image of America was never fixed. Depending on who was speaking, America could be either fascinating or appalling, a repository of hope or horror" (5). Even as Europeans look down on America, they flock to its movies, love its music, and imitate its business practices.

More than anything, perhaps, Americans tire Europeans. They have so much drive and energy, such a sense of mission and purpose—the mission being to create the perfect society, that new Eden mentioned above—that they leave the average European fatigued and breathless. It's not that Europeans don't dream (on occasion) of a more perfect world, but only that they are more realistic about the prospects. They did their best, in a way, with the Enlightenment, which was indeed a great leap forward for Western civilization; now they need to rest. Let America, young and dynamic and full of promise, have her turn.

The dominant tone in European pronouncements on America seems to be that of the judgmental parent. To Europeans, Americans are like unruly teenagers, with all the usual mannerisms, good and bad, of those mixed-up youths: they are innocent, naive, and completely lacking in self-discipline; loud, full of energy, and optimistic; they have very little self-confidence and care far too much about what other people think. They can also be extremely honest and thoroughly engaging.

Americans' Attitudes toward Europeans

Toward Europeans, as toward all people, Americans make

every effort to remain open and accepting. This doesn't mean that Americans don't find the French arrogant, let's say (which they do), or Germans blunt, but only that they try not to think any less of or look down on the French or Germans for their behavior. They allow them their behavior, in other words, even if they don't appreciate it. This uncritical acceptance, incidentally—the live-and-let-live philosophy—deeply disturbs many Europeans; to them it means Americans have no core beliefs, nothing they're willing to stand up for. But to Americans this attitude is merely the expression of genuine tolerance, one of the core values of their society. Indeed, if there's one thing the normally accepting, uncritical Americans *cannot* in fact accept about Europeans, it is their apparent lack of tolerance, and in particular what Americans see as their air of superiority.

Try as they might to be nonjudgmental, Americans do have a few opinions about Europeans, and as it turns out, Americans are almost as conflicted toward Europeans as Europeans are toward them. On the one hand, Americans like to disassociate themselves from Europe, from the home of the bankrupt ideologies and oppressive social structures that called America into being in the first place. This view supports the popular American notion (noted elsewhere) that the United States was something quite new on the world scene, a nation and an ideology utterly unlike anything that had come before. If people believe this about their country, then they will want to distance themselves from any ancestors or forebears, from any precedents. Something so unique, after all, must by definition be unprecedented.

But even as they eschew all things European—Europe is the problem to which America is the solution—Americans crave the approval of Europeans. Europe is still the motherland, after all, and even if it wasn't always such a good parent, the tie of blood is strong. "Toward Europe," Daniel Boorstin has written,

> we have felt all the attractions and repulsions of Oedipus. Only by denying our parent can we be-come a truly independent New World; yet we can-not help feeling that the New World is the fulfill-ment of a European dream. We are both a happy non-Europe and a happy afterlife of Europe. Eu-rope is both our beloved "mother country" and the pernicious source of all "alien ideologies." We owe to her our religion, our common law, our ideal of constitutionalism; but also the ancient menaces of aristocracy, feudalism, and monopoly, and the mod-ern menace of communism.
>
> Few peoples have been so obsessed by a parental image…. Most European nations do not know from where their first settlers came. We of all modern peoples are dominated by the specter of known for-eign ancestors. (1976, 11, 12)

Europeans tend to intimidate Americans and cause them to doubt themselves. There may be something of the child seeking the approval of the parent here, but there is also something else. Europeans exhibit a degree of self-confidence, for example, which few Americans can match, and of which most are in awe. Even when they're wrong about something—indeed, especially when they've got it wrong—Europeans feel not the slightest twinge of self-doubt. They may have gotten it wrong this time, one is made to understand, but that's merely because of circum-stances, not insufficient wisdom. Europeans don't *always* have to be right to know they're *essentially* right. If Europeans are so sure of things, it's no doubt because they have seen it all before, many times, in fact, and are not easily impressed. This "depth of culture," as Allister Sparks puts it, gives Europeans a certain "assured maturity" quite lacking in their American cousins (1999, 72). Americans, for all their bluster, tend to fall silent before the seemingly effortless self-assurance of the typical European.

Americans greatly admire the achievements of European culture, the great art and the great ideas, and cheerfully accept their own inferior status in this regard. They know they're not as sophisticated or refined as Europeans—that they are in effect works in progress, culturally and intellectually, rather than finished products—and they will often defer to European opinion or argument because it must be more informed. In short, Americans accept that Europeans will on occasion be patronizing and condescending and try not to take it too seriously. It's the duty of elders, after all, to prescribe to youth, and the duty of youth to grin and bear it.

* * *

In closing, we have a final word of caution for readers. It's not true, alas, that having now spent a few hours reading about European/American cultural differences, all of your cross-cultural interactions are going to go smoothly, that the irritating things Europeans or Americans do are no longer going to irritate you. The truth is that information or knowledge, which is what you have gained by reading this book, is a necessary but by no means a sufficient condition for changing attitudes and behavior. To put it another way, in reading this book you may have been *alerted* to various cultural differences, but that doesn't mean you've

gotten used to them. That only comes with time and experience.

Meanwhile, even if the odd things Europeans and
Americans do continue to irritate or confuse you, at least
now you will begin to understand why they do those things.
Knowing why people from other cultures behave the way
they do—and especially knowing that their behavior makes
sense to them even if it makes none to you—is the first
and most important step in successfully crossing cultures.

Bibliography

Ardagh, John. 1995. *Germany and the Germans*. 3d ed. London: Penguin Books.

Asselin, Gilles, and Ruth Mastron. 2001. *Au Contraire! Figuring Out the French*. Yarmouth, ME: Intercultural Press.

Atkinson, Rick. 1994. "Collapse of a German Construction King." *Washington Post*, 17 April, D1.

Barsoux, Jean-Louis, and Peter Lawrence. 1997. "The Nature of Work Relations." In *Exploring Management across the World*, edited by David J. Hickson. London: Penguin Books.

———. 1991. "The Making of a French Manager." *Harvard Business Review*, July–August, 60.

Barzini, Luigi. 1983. *The Europeans*. London: Penguin Books.

Boorstin, Daniel J. 1976. *America and the Image of Europe: Reflections on American Thought.* Gloucester, MA: Peter Smith.

———. 1965. *The Americans: The National Experience.* New York: Random House.

———. 1958. *The Americans: The Colonial Experience.* New York: Random House.

Bryson, Bill. 1995. *Notes from a Small Island.* New York: Avon Books.

Buruma, Ian. 1998. *Anglomania: A European Love Affair.* New York: Random House.

Carroll, Raymonde. 1988. *Cultural Misunderstandings: The French-American Experience.* Chicago: University of Chicago Press.

Dale, Reginald. 1999. "Europe's Big Entrepreneurial Gap." *International Herald Tribune,* 20 July.

Degler, Carl N. 1984. *Out of Our Past: The Forces that Shaped Modern America.* New York: Harper & Row.

DeVita, Philip R., and James D. Armstrong. 1993. *Distant Mirrors: America as a Foreign Culture.* Belmont, CA: Wadsworth Publishing.

Djursaa, Malene. 1994. "North European Business Cultures." *European Management Journal* 12, no. 2, Oxford: Pergamon.

Drozdiak, William. 1998. "The German Status Quo." *Washington Post,* 16 March, A13.

Flamini, Roland. 1997. *Passport Germany: Your Pocket Guide to German Business, Customs & Etiquette.* San Rafael, CA: World Trade Press.

Foster, Dean. 1999. Personal interview cited in Shawn E. Quill, "A Failed ET/MCI Mega-Merger." Unpublished paper. American University. School of International Service. 12 May.

Foster, George M. 1965. "Peasant Society and the Image of Limited Good." *American Anthropologist* 67, no. 2, April, 296.

Gannon, Martin J. and Associates. 1994. *Understanding Global Cultures: Metaphorical Journeys Through 17 Countries.* Thousand Oaks, CA: Sage.

Gibbs, Paul. 1992. *Doing Business in the European Community.* London: Kogan/Page.

Gramont, Sanche de. 1969. *The French: Portrait of a People.* New York: G. P. Putnam's Sons.

Hall, Edward T., and Mildred Reed Hall. 1990. *Understanding Cultural Differences.* Yarmouth, ME: Intercultural Press.

Hargraves, Orin. 1997. *Living and Working Abroad: London.* Singapore: Times Books.

Harper, Timothy. 1997. *Passport United Kingdom: Your Pocket Guide to British Business, Customs & Etiquette.* San Rafael, CA: World Trade Press.

Harris, Philip R., and Robert T. Moran. 1987. *Managing Cultural Differences.* Houston: Gulf Publishing.

Hendrickson, Paul. 1998. "Witness to the Unimaginable." *Washington Post,* 15 November, Sec. F7.

Hickson, David J., ed. 1997. *Exploring Management across the World.* London: Penguin Books.

Hickson, David J., and Derek S. Pugh. 1995. *Management Worldwide.* London: Penguin Books.

Hill, Richard. 1995. *WeEuropeans.* Brussels: Europublications.

———. 1994. *EuroManagers & Martians*. Brussels: Europublications.

Hofstede, Geert. 1988. *Culture's Consequences: International Differences in Work-Related Values*. Abridged ed. Beverly Hills, CA: Sage.

Hymowitz, Carol. 2000. "Companies Go Global, but Many Managers Just Don't Travel Well." *The Wall Street Journal*, 15 August, B1.

Ibrahim, Youssef. 1996. "We Can't Do Business, the Dons Tell Big Donor." *New York Times*, 26 November, Sec. A4.

James, Henry. 1986. *The Ambassadors*. London: Penguin.

Jones, Howard Mumford. 1968. *O Strange New World: American Culture: The Formative Years*. New York: Viking.

Joseph, Nadine. 1997. *Passport France: Your Pocket Guide to French Business, Customs & Etiquette*. San Rafael, CA: World Trade Press.

Keegan, John. 1997. "Deadly as the Male." *Washington Post*, 11 May, Book World, 4.

Lawrence, Peter, and Vincent Edwards. 2000. *Management in Western Europe*. London: Macmillan Press.

Lisle, Leanda de. 1997. "Great Minds...." *The Spectator*, 22 March, 52.

Lord, Richard. 1998. *Culture Shock! Succeed in Business. Germany*. Portland, OR: Graphic Arts Center Publishing.

———. 1996. *Culture Shock! Germany: A Guide to Customs and Etiquette*. Portland, OR: Graphic Arts Center Publishing.

McElroy, John Harmon. 1999. *American Beliefs: What Keeps a Big Country and a Diverse People United.* Chicago: Ivan R. Dee.

McGinn, Daniel, and Stefan Theil. 1999. "Steady Hands: Will the DaimlerChrysler Combination Succeed? Ask Middle Management." *Newsweek International,* 12 April, 51, 52.

Miall, Anthony. 1998. *The Xenophobe's Guide to the English.* Horsham, West Sussex: Ravette Publishing.

Miller, Stuart. 1990. *Understanding Europeans.* Santa Fe, NM: John Muir.

Mole, John. 1995. *Mind Your Manners: Managing Business Cultures in Europe.* London: Nicholas Brealey Publishing.

Moran, Robert T. 1992. *Doing Business in Europe.* Oxford: Heinemann.

Nees, Greg. 2000. *Germany: Unraveling an Enigma.* Yarmouth, ME: Intercultural Press.

North, Peter. 1999. *Culture Shock: Success Secrets to Maximize Business in Britain.* Singapore: Times Editions.

Pakenham, Thomas. 1991. *The Scramble for Africa: White Man's Conquest of the Dark Continent from 1876 to 1912.* New York: Avon Books.

Payer, Lynn. 1989. *Medicine and Culture: Varieties of Treatment in the United States, England, West Germany, and France.* New York: Penguin Books.

Pells, Richard. 1997. *Not Like Us: How Europeans Have Loved, Hated, and Transformed American Culture Since World War II.* New York: Basic Books.

Platt, Polly. 1995. *French or Foe?: Getting the Most out of Visiting, Living and Working in France*. Skokie, IL: Culture Crossings.

Randlesome, Colin, et al. 1995. *Business Cultures in Europe*. Oxford: Butterworth-Heinemann.

Reid, T. R. 1999. "What Price Britain." *Washington Post*, 28 September, A19.

Rosenblum, Mort. 1988. *Mission to Civilize: The French Way*. New York: Anchor Press Doubleday.

Sparks, Allister. 1999. "Mandela's South Africa—and After." *Wilson Quarterly*, Spring, 72.

Spoto, Donald. 1995. *The Decline and Fall of the House of Windsor*. New York: Simon & Schuster.

Stewart, Edward C., and Milton J. Bennett. 1991. *American Cultural Patterns: A Cross-Cultural Perspective*. 2d ed. Yarmouth, ME: Intercultural Press.

Swardson, Anne. 2000. "Air France Suspends English Experiment." *Washington Post*, 7 April.

Tocqueville, Alexis de. 1984. *Democracy in America*. New York: Penguin Books.

Twain, Mark. 1895. *The Innocents Abroad*. Hartford, CT: American Publishing Company.

Wolin, Richard. 1999. "The Anti-American Revolution." *New Republic*, 17 and 24 August, 35.

Yapp, Peter, ed. 1988. *The Traveler's Dictionary of Quotations: Who Said What, About Where?* London: Routledge.

Yardley, Jonathan. 1999. *Washington Post*, 6 June, Book World, 2.

Zeldin, Theodore. 1996. *The French*. New York: Kodansha International.

Index of Key Concepts
(listed by Dialogue Number)

The French

The Germans

The Americans